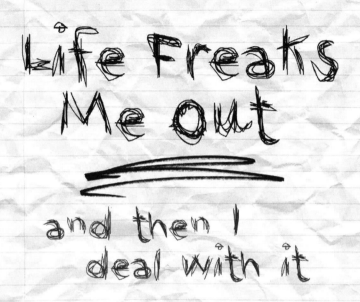

Life Freaks Me out

and then I deal with it

K.L. Hong

Search Institute
INSTITUTE

A Search Institute Publication

Life Freaks Me Out:
And Then I Deal with It

10 9 8 7 6 5 4 3
Printed on acid-free paper in the
United States of America

Search Institute
615 First Avenue Northeast, Suite 125
Minneapolis, MN 55413
www.search-institute.org
612-376-8955 • 800-888-7828

credits
editors: Jennifer Griffin-Wiesner,
        Tenessa Gemelke
book design: Cathy Spengler
production coordinator: Mary Ellen Buscher

**library of congress cataloging-in-
publication data**
Hong, K. L.
  Life freaks me out : and then I deal with it /
K.L. Hong.
      p. cm.
  ISBN 1-57482-856-8 (pbk. : alk. paper)
  1. Teenagers—Conduct of life.
  2. Hong, K. L.
  I. Title.
  BJ1661.H66 2005
  158'.0835—dc22
                        2005009461

· Contents ·

To John Eggers, my teacher,

and to Ted, Mariah, Sonora, Thor, and Evan,

with love

If Someone Else Gave You This Book, Why Should You Read It?

Because I wrote it for you.

I wrote it for you if you're a young person who's filled with questions about life and love and relationships and work, about finding your way in the world and making sense of it all.

I wrote it for you if you're a teacher or a parent or a youth worker or anyone else who's trying to help a young person find her or his way in the world and who might be grateful for some reminders about what it's like to be a teenager from someone who hasn't forgotten.

I wrote the truest, most honest book I could write—from one human to another—about what life was like when I was a teenager and what it's like now, and how learning about life started back then and continues today.

I wrote it because I wanted to send you a message from the other side—from the other side of my teenage years, from the other side of my struggles and confusions—to help us find a common language and a bridge across the generations.

I wrote it with openness and honesty, revealing much of what I've done, thought, felt, succeeded at, messed up, and repaired in my life, when I was a teenager and since then, and how I've come through it all to a good place.

I wrote it in the hope that by traveling with me as a companion on part of my life journey, you will discover an understanding or a tale or a phrase that helps you find your own daily truths and your own path to courage, love, and joy.

—K.L. Hong

I Choose to Believe

I choose to believe that there is a reason why this book has come into your hands.

I choose to believe that you, especially, are at an important place and time in your life journey. At this moment and in the years to come, no matter your age or gender or circumstances, you can use something that is written here.

I know you have questions—everyone does. They may be questions about feelings and desires, about money and how to get more. Or perhaps you wonder about work, school, and activities. Maybe you're trying to figure out something about friends, dating, love, marriage, sex, changing bodies, or drinking and using drugs. For most of us, different days bring different questions . . . and sometimes the same old ones, too.

This book is all about questions. It is about the bigger questions that lie underneath the specific ones—the questions that really matter, the questions *life* is asking *you:* What is really important to you? Who are you and where are you going (and why)? What is life calling you to be and do? And it's about how I discovered those questions as a teenager, and how I've found my own answers during my life so far.

what is life calling you to be and do?

I've been finding my own answers for quite a while now. I believe that when you know how to find your own answers to the bigger questions, you'll discover, as I have, that the answers to the others start to become clear, too.

Let me tell you a story.

When I was 15, back in 1975, I was a junior at Lincoln High School in Sioux Falls, South Dakota. From the outside, I was a skinny girl in low-slung bell-bottom jeans, with long golden hair, a straightened-teeth smile beneath a larger-than-necessary nose, good grades, and a few close—though not terribly popular—friends. I guess I looked pretty "normal," even though I was one of the youngest kids in my class (I had started school early). My friend, Mark, says that to him, I seemed as if I had the world figured out. From the inside, though, everything was awful and I was terribly unhappy.

School seemed pointless, despite my ability to get decent grades; classes were boring; it was one long day after another of feeling like a failure. Just making it through the hallways crowded with noise and teasing felt brutal. Nobody, it seemed, understood me. The activities I had enjoyed in junior high—gymnastics, chorus, playing musical instruments—turned into fierce competition in high school rather than things to do for fun, and I quit them all. I didn't know how to find my way into the popular cliques, and I felt lost and lonely in my class of 700 students. I wanted more than anything to belong to a group—and the only group I found that seemed open to accepting me for myself was the druggie crowd.

Well, I was miserable. My parents didn't seem to understand what I was going through, and in between their fighting with each other, we often fought—over what I was wearing, where I was going, who I was with, what I'd be doing, when I'd be home. It would probably have helped if I could have turned to some wise person I could talk with and trust—maybe a teacher or my pastor or a school counselor—but I didn't; I was so unhappy that I couldn't look up and around enough to see whether someone might be standing by. I just endured and did the best I could in my daily life and dragged myself to school day after day.

The whole situation got worse and worse until finally I threw an absolute fit at home and told my parents I was going to quit school. I screamed and cried and said, "If you want me to go to school, you'd better find me a different one to go to—the private Catholic school across town, anything, but I'm not going back!"

Not the most mature discussion, I suppose, but at least I was honest, and they heard me. I was lucky; they found a place for me to go. (Homeschooling was not a legal option back then.) We discovered that some teachers at the regular high school—they didn't like it, either!—were starting a smaller alternative high school in a neighboring building. I got into that school—the Compass School—for my senior year, and I don't think I'm exaggerating when I say it saved my life.

Suddenly, instead of being forced to go to required classes in a huge school, the other 60 students and I could choose what classes we wanted to take, if any, and for the rest of the time we made contracts with the three teachers—our "advisors"—to learn what we wanted to. We kept weekly journals, did volunteer work in the community, and had group and individual meetings with the advisors. We had freedom to read and explore, we could learn things that seemed relevant to us, we had responsibility for our own time and our own learning, and we had the space and support to start finding out about ourselves.

And, perhaps most important of all, I had my advisor, John Eggers. He was a big bear of a man at 6 feet 6 inches with dark curly hair and a bushy beard, fierce eyebrows, strong, broad shoulders, a quiet sense of humor, and twinkling eyes. He taught me more than any other teacher before or since . . . and it's what he taught me that led me to want and be able to write this book.

I'll never forget my surprise when I got to school one morning and walked into his office for our weekly one-on-one meeting. When

I closed his office door, I saw that on the back of it he had put up a handmade poster. At the top he'd written the words WHAT I BELIEVE, and then had listed numbers down the left side. He had written in statements for numbers 1, 2, and 3. I only remember what number 3 said: LOVE IS NICE, BUT IT'S NOT NECESSARY.

"Love is nice, but it's not necessary?!"

I swung around. "Is that a quote from someone?" I demanded. (Mark says he remembers me as having a "potentially savaging tongue.") John didn't take it personally, though. He just answered, "No, it's something I believe is true that I figured out for myself."

"Do you *really* believe that? Isn't love the most important thing in life?" This question came from my unpopular then-16-year-old self, who desperately wanted a boyfriend.

And John said, "Yes, I really believe that. It's nice to have a good relationship, but there are things that are more necessary, like being honest with yourself, finding out what you want to do with your life, learning how to be your own best friend."

I don't remember the rest of our conversation that morning. I do recall being amazed that a person could just write down her or his own ideas and turn them into quotations to live by! And I remember that he encouraged me to start looking harder for what *I* believed and gave me a list of quotations to get me going. A bunch of us students looked at them together that afternoon and made posters of the ones we thought were the best. I picked one from Omar Khayyam, a Persian mathematician and poet who lived a thousand years ago: I MYSELF AM HEAVEN AND HELL. That seemed so true to me, because I was experiencing within myself the hellishness of confusion and fear and doubt, and also, sometimes, the wonder and joy of being confident enough to say what I believed and to act on those beliefs and have it turn out right.

There is more than one kind of truth. There is Truth with a capital T, the big spiritual kind about the deepest issues of life: whether there is a higher power, why there is evil in the world, whether there is life after death. I was and have ever since been on that spiritual journey, too. But the truths I learned about that day are about finding my way in the world and making sense of the daily stuff of relationships and choices and challenges. And the most important things I learned that day were that I could find my own truths, that there were lots of places to look for them, and that, if I didn't find them out in the world, I could find them within myself.

I've been working on that for almost 30 years, and am still working on it, with help from other people and also with a lot of struggle through making mistakes and learning the hard way. Each of the truths I've discovered has helped me find my own right answers to all kinds of questions about myself and life, what to do and how to do it and who to do it with, about what I want and what I need and what I'd better do without. And when I look back, I see that much of what I believe to be true now had its beginnings in the experiences of my teenage years.

Consider this book my "What I Believe" poster. In it, I've put into writing 10 of the best, most useful truths I believe in, truths I've found or created for myself during my 46 years of life so far. I share the stories of how they came to me and what they mean for me. I state them in the ways that seem powerful to me—not with any kind of authority except my own experience—in the hope that they will help *you* to seek and find your own daily truths, to discover and revel in your answers to the questions life is asking you.

· 1 ·
You Are the Most Powerful Person in Your Life

When I was at the Compass School, we had weekly meetings with about ten kids and one advisor. During these group sessions, we talked about life and issues that came up in our volunteer work and about our journal writing and contract learning activities. It was a new experience for me to talk about things in a group like that, and, being rather shy and private in some ways, I didn't always like it much.

I remember I came to school one day in a really bad mood. I had been fighting with my parents about their rules, and how I felt that they were trying to control my life, and how I didn't think they understood how important it was for me to be with my friends. I'm sure now that when I walked into Group, everyone could see from my face and body language that I was upset and angry. I didn't care. I wanted them to know it; I wanted everyone to know it.

I wound up talking with irritation about one of the requirements we had to meet, saying how stupid I thought it was and how hard it was to make it work out. After the meeting, my advisor, John, asked to talk to me in his office. "Oh, geez, now what?!" I thought. I already felt as if everyone was against me; I didn't need this.

Not being able to think of a way out of it, I stomped into his office and threw myself down in the chair.

"What?"

He looked at me for a minute, preparing, I assumed, to put me in my place. But instead of yelling, he asked me what was going on that was making me so upset. I started telling him about that morning's fight with my parents and how awful everything was. As I talked, I felt myself calming down a little—at least *someone* was willing to listen to me—but I still didn't know why he called me into his office. When I ran out of words, I slouched back in the chair and stared at the ugly gray carpet, expecting a repeat of the fight with my parents: telling me why I was wrong, why my parents were right, and that my feelings were screwed up, and probably that I had talked too much in Group. But John surprised me. Instead of lecturing, he told me something I've remembered my whole life.

"You know, Kay, I don't think you realize how powerful you are."

I lifted my eyes from the floor to stare at him. I felt like the least powerful person in the world. Everyone was controlling me, I couldn't do what I wanted to after school or on weekends, everything I tried to do or wanted didn't work out, I was unhappy and I blamed it on my family and my school and politicians and everyone else. I thought he was nuts.

"When you came into Group this morning, the rest of us were already there. You came in angry and negative, and that affected everyone. They were watching you, responding to you. On other days, when you come in with a positive attitude, the group responds to that, too. You have a strong, intense spirit and the ability to speak your thoughts and feelings. I want you to realize that you can *choose* whether that influence is a good one or a bad one."

I was speechless. I had never seen myself as having power in the group, having influence. I always felt as if the group existed and I just had to try to find a way to fit in with what was already going on. I also assumed that was only going to work once in a while. I was used to feeling separate, apart, different, not good enough. It had never occurred to me that I contributed to what the group was, that my being there was part of creating it, and that I could decide for myself what kind of contribution I was going to make.

I felt something inside me change at that moment. It was a strange feeling, as if a part of me expanded and grew deeper, like a plant sprouted and put out some roots.

Seeing Myself in a New Way

That day I saw myself for the first time from the *outside*. Suddenly, I could imagine how I must have looked, flouncing into the meeting room, displaying my anger and waving it around the room like a flag. I was always getting so mad at everyone else for not being responsible for the ways their behavior affected me; I scrutinized everyone else's looks and actions, attitudes and words, and criticized them for being hypocrites, but I had never taken that same kind of hard look at myself and my own actions and attitudes. Wow.

I've never forgotten that feeling, that realization. And over the years I've come to think of that moment as the time when I first really started growing up for real, when I first started to become *myself*.

Just Beginning

Our whole lives are a long journey of becoming ourselves, becoming responsible for our own lives, becoming whole within ourselves in body, mind, and spirit. When we are babies, we are utterly dependent on grown-ups to care for us. As little children, we progress to walking, talking, feeding ourselves. As we go to school, we see a bit more of the world, learning about how people live in our coun-

try and in other countries, about ideas and theories, about relationships, about our bodies and our sexuality, about work. When it's
time to leave school and actually start to "travel" on our own, we
may have a graduation ceremony or move out of our parents' home.
And there's a part of us that thinks, "There, I'm done with all that,
now I can start living!"

But what most of us find out is that we're only just beginning,
in our late teens and early twenties, the journey to becoming ourselves. We crave independence—having our own car or going places
on our own, finding a job, moving to another town or city—and are
convinced that once we are free to do these things, life will be good.
But we bump up against so many things we can't control: the boss
who doesn't hire us, the landlord who won't rent to us, the other
people in our lives who don't behave the way we want them to. And
we face decisions to be made that sometimes bring unexpected
and undesirable consequences, like driving home from a bar after
drinking and winding up in a crash. And we often resist being solely
responsible, blaming others for our situations—oh, those irritating
parents, bosses, landlords, other drivers, boyfriends and girlfriends.

Suddenly, the idea of being responsible becomes a lot less
appealing than it first seemed to be, when we were still living by
the rules of parents and school. What I found, however, once I
accepted that I couldn't control other people's emotions and actions
and that I had to take the good with the bad in life, is that responsibility is more powerful than I imagined.

A few years ago, I learned a trick about understanding power
and responsibility that has helped me a lot. I was taking an anger-
management class, and the trainer had us draw two circles, one kind
of large, and the other smaller and inside the first. First, he asked us
to label the inside circle with our name. He said, "That circle is you;
write in your emotions right now, your attitudes about life, your

recent choices." Next, he had us write in the space around our little circle the things that bothered us about the world and other people, the frustrations of our life. Here's what mine looked like:

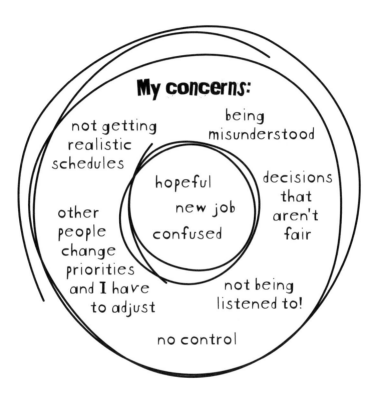

My concerns:

not getting
realistic
schedules

being
misunderstood

hopeful
new job
confused

decisions
that
aren't
fair

other
people
change
priorities
and I have
to adjust

not being
listened to!

no control

Then he said, "Now, look at those two circles; the little one is all the stuff you can control." And I realized that what is in my control is also what is my responsibility to deal with. When you feel as if you are powerless, maybe you'd find it helpful to try this approach. Here are two circles for you to use:

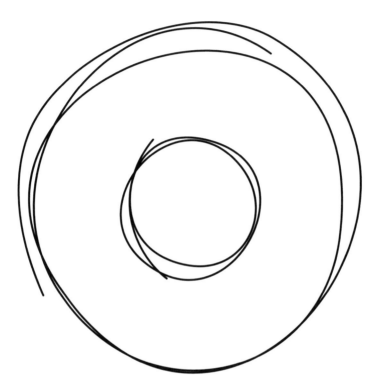

The thing is, as I keep on becoming my adult self, I have wanted
to be more and more in charge of my own life. To do that, though,
I have had to stop trying to control everything that happens to me.
I can't make people like me or treat me right; I can't make everything
work out the way I want it to. Sometimes that has left me feeling
betrayed and angry, or weak and powerless. But the flip side of the
coin is that when I let go of the other stuff, I see that I am the only
one who has the power to control—to take responsibility for—
myself and my attitudes, my choices and my actions. Other people
can't decide for me what I'm going to think, or do, or believe. Even
though the responsibility can be scary, it's also exciting to know I
have ultimate power in that small circle. The way I say it to myself

sometimes is, "I get to choose, and I have to choose." And I say that second part, the "I have to choose," because if I don't, I'm giving away the only power that's truly mine.

Growing My Own Command Center

I wasn't the only kid at the Compass School who fought with her or his parents. In fact, many people start having conflicts with their parents and teachers and other adults around the time they become teenagers. One of the coolest things I've learned lately is one of the reasons why that is so, and I learned it from reading articles and books about brain research.

People used to think that a person's brain was pretty much done "growing" by age 5 or 6; after that point, it was just a matter of "filling it up" with stuff. You know that idea; it's the one that seems true in some teachers' classrooms, where you're just supposed to memorize a bunch of dates and names and facts that don't seem to connect with anything. There was an idea that all people were supposed to develop in the same way and go through certain stages of development toward maturity. And adults figured that teenagers were just being stubborn, rebellious, or scatterbrained when they didn't behave the way they were supposed to or control their feelings or remember the eight chores they were supposed to do before dinner.

But recent research on how brains develop has brought new clarity to this time of life. We now know that while lots of important brain growth does happen in early childhood, there are several other big brain-growth "spurts" later—and guess when they happen? During the teen years.

There is a part of the adult brain, called the prefrontal cortex, that doesn't develop until adolescence and isn't done maturing until you're about 20 or 21. It's what researchers sometimes call the *executive* part, because it's what allows you to make more careful decisions, to keep all your tasks and responsibilities in mind, to sort through duty and conscience and control. Turns out it is true that adults and teens are different—not quite different species, but ones with different brains! That explains a lot.

turns out that adults and teens have different brains!

It's part of why conflict with parents or whoever else is raising you is common when you're 14, 15, 16, 17, 18, 19, 20. For so many years, those people have basically acted as that decision-making part of your brain, the part you haven't yet fully developed. They have acted as your commander, your reminder, your leader, your conscience, your control panel. And now you're beginning to create that in yourself, and you don't always want it from the outside anymore.

Just like the rest of our bodies, our brains need to be cared for and used in order to get stronger. I believe that each time I experienced my own power, each time I felt inside of me that new sense of something growing or taking root, I was literally making or strengthening a new brain path. And when *you* spend time figuring things out, trying to think about your ideas and emotions and process them and choose how to act, you are exercising this developing part of your brain. A psychologist named David Walsh, who has written a book about brain development, calls the process "blossoming and pruning." Your brain develops so many paths during this amazing time that it makes more than it can actually keep. The paths that are used most frequently tend to stick with you; the rest are "cut away" to make room for others.

This explains, in part, why it's best to not smoke, drink alcohol, or use drugs during your teen years. The chemicals in them change how your brain physically works and make it harder for you to do the things you need to in order to help it grow. It's also easier to become addicted during your teens, because your brain develops paths that learn to depend on the drugs. Wish I'd known this before I started smoking at age 15.

Creating the Meaning of My Life

So what's the point of all this talk about brains, power, and responsibility? The point is that these ideas have been very important in helping me create my life and the meaning of my life. Maybe you'll find some of this information helpful, too.

I wondered a lot when I was a teenager about what I was supposed to do with my life and what the meaning of it all was (sometimes I still do). The difference between then and now is that I used to think that when I didn't know what I was supposed to do with my life, somehow I would just "find" the answer—as if the meaning of life was out there somewhere waiting to be picked up like a pebble on the sidewalk, put in my pocket, and then I'd have it.

When I truly started to believe in my own power, in my own ability to take control of my life and of myself, I started thinking in a different way. Now I know that I can create my own meaning, my own purpose. And the way I do it is by starting with a truth— sometimes the truth is discovered in my own thoughts, or I find it by reading and looking around me and talking to other people— and then making it real by using it in my daily life. I've come across three great sayings about putting truths into action to create the meanings of my life. One is really positive, one more negative, and one more neutral. For me, a different one works in different situations, depending on what's going on with me.

We all walk in darkness, and each of us must turn on our own light. I can't remember where I heard or read this saying; I just have it written down in an old journal. The idea of needing to turn on my own light reminds me that I'm not alone in feeling in the dark sometimes. We all get confused, we all feel as if we are "in the dark" some days. And we all have the experience as we grow up of having to leave behind childhood, when we were taken care of by others, and learn to take care of ourselves.

When I was a teenager, a popular rock song by a guy named Alice Cooper was a kind of anthem for many of us who grew up in the seventies. The refrain was "I'm 18! I get confused every day!" I've been remembering that song lately, finding the screaming chorus running through my mind as I'm trying to solve a problem or process a strange conversation with someone. Nowadays, I'm better at dealing with the times of confusion—when I feel as if I'm walking in darkness—because I've seen them come so many times. Even so, I still can find myself mixed up and discouraged and thinking, "No one told me life would be this hard!"

Fortunately, we each have the power to light our own way, and no one else can turn the light on for us: not a boyfriend or girlfriend, not a parent or teacher, not a boss or a friend or anyone else (although they can sometimes help by "pointing us to the switch"). That means to me that being passive about life is not right; it's a "cop-out," bailing out on my own power and my own responsibility to choose. I can put off decisions, and I can let other people make decisions for me, but eventually, it all comes back to me. And when I feel as though I'm in a dim cave of confusion and the Alice Cooper chorus is starting to get stuck in my head again, it's up to me to find out how to turn on the light.

If you want to keep getting what you're getting, keep doing what you're doing. I found this saying on a refrigerator magnet at an office where I worked for a short while during my twenties. There are times when I find myself really frustrated— mentally beating my head against the wall about dealing with a friend I can't seem to agree with or a life that isn't interesting enough or an unhappiness that just won't go away. That's when it's useful to think: IF YOU WANT TO KEEP GETTING WHAT YOU'RE GETTING, KEEP DOING WHAT YOU'RE DOING. My brother, Todd, told me the same thing happens to him sometimes, and he uses a different quote, one from Albert Einstein: "Insanity is doing the same thing over and over again and expecting a different result."

Here's how it works for me: When I hit that wall of frustration, that sense that I'm not getting what I want, especially from another person, I remember this saying, especially the part about "keep doing what you're doing."

That usually gets me started thinking about just what it is I have been doing. It reminds me that when I feel as if nothing is working, I should take a look to see whether I've really tried everything. It turns my view from outside to inside, from the big circle to the little circle, and quietly suggests that maybe there is something else, something more or different I could do. And it helps me pause long enough to consider whether what I've been wanting to get is reasonable.

I remember once feeling very bothered that a friend of mine in high school was always late. Our other friend, Terri, and I would expect her at a certain time, and it would be an hour or more later that she would finally arrive. Or Terri and I would go over to pick her up at her house, and instead of a quick hello to her folks and a fast getaway, we'd wind up sitting there impatiently while she dug through her closet for different clothes to wear. At the time, it felt to us that we had tried lots of different ways to get what we wanted, which was for her to be on time. We tried calling her in advance to urge her to start getting ready early. We tried telling her that the time for a party was an hour earlier than it really was. We tried telling her we were angry with her about it.

Had I known this saying then, I might have said to myself, Well, maybe there's something different I should be doing, or maybe there's something different I should be wanting. Instead of trying to change her, I could have tried to accept her being a not very punctual person and looked for ways to deal with it or be more patient. This approach might have opened my mind to some alternatives, like keeping a book or crossword puzzle handy when she was going to come by, so I could amuse myself during the waiting time; or deciding not to take rides from or give rides to her, but to meet at parties and other events instead.

maybe there is something else, something more or different i could do.

If I had known this saying when I was a teenager, it might have helped me do a few other things differently or better, too. I might have realized a lot sooner that doing drugs and drinking weren't actually making me happy and started looking for some other kinds of activities and hobbies. I might have made a point, when I was feeling stuck and powerless, of seeking help from someone older and wiser than myself instead of continuing to struggle with it alone. I might have noticed that certain friends weren't actually very good friends and decided to start figuring out how to give myself the good attention I needed.

Nowadays, I use this saying to help me in my friendships, in my daily chores and tasks, and even in my work—whenever I find myself feeling frustrated and starting to blame other people for my disappointments and irritations. The point is that when you're stuck on the same situation, and you think to yourself that you've tried everything, you haven't tried everything. But what you might need to try is changing something about yourself, your wants, and how you operate.

Things aren't always as they seem. When I'm angry, when I feel as if life is unfair, when I catch myself feeling passionately that other people are wrong and only my way is right, if I'm lucky, I'll hear this saying in my mind.

It's a common one, but the illustration of it that sticks in my mind is from the movie *The Karate Kid.* Have you ever seen it? (I've watched it at least eight or ten times; it's one of my favorites from when I was in my early twenties, a true '80s classic.) The story is about a teenage boy, Daniel, who moves to Los Angeles and struggles with getting along in his new school and with not having any friends except the maintenance man for his apartment building. As a new kid, he winds up getting picked on and teased and eventually beaten up by some bullies who take karate. When he discovers that the maintenance man, Mr. Miyagi, is an expert in karate, Daniel asks to be taught karate so he can defend himself. Mr. Miyagi agrees to teach him, and Daniel arrives at his house the next day ready for his first lesson.

But instead of starting to teach him karate moves, Mr. Miyagi sets him to work doing chores, including cleaning and waxing each of his five vintage cars. He gives Daniel very specific instructions about the hand motions to use, telling him to use a big clockwise arm movement to put the wax on, and a big counterclockwise arm movement to rub the wax off.

Well, Daniel thinks it's weird, but he does it. He works really hard, and thinks that when he's done, he'll finally get some lessons. But all that happens is that Mr. Miyagi thanks him for his work, and the next day has him paint the big fence that goes all around his yard! Again, he gives him very specific instructions about how to use a flowing wrist motion as he moves the paintbrush up and down, over and over, while he's painting. The third day, Daniel is assigned the task of sanding the boards of the long walkway in Mr. Miyagi's Japanese-style garden.

Well, the longer he works, the more upset Daniel gets. He thinks Mr. Miyagi is maybe crazy, or else is just messing with his mind. Finally, he rebels and tells Mr. Miyagi firmly and angrily that all this work is dumb and that it won't help him learn karate and he's not going to do it anymore.

That's when something amazing happens. Mr. Miyagi tells him gently that things are not always as they seem. He begins to show him some basic karate moves and demonstrates to him that the arm movements he has been repeating during all the chores are actually the same movements that counter attacks. After Daniel practices a little bit with him, Mr. Miyagi begins a series of attacking moves toward him, and Daniel is able to deflect them all. The realization of what a fine teacher Mr. Miyagi is shows in the wonder on Daniel's face during one of the most striking moments in the movie. Daniel suddenly realizes that not everything is the way it seems to him, that he doesn't really know it all, and that sometimes, to be successful in your life, you have to trust your teacher and wait to see how things turn out.

This saying reminds me that sometimes I can choose to wait and do nothing for awhile, especially when that is the advice of someone I trust. Instead of blaming others, getting caught up in my anger, or being too quick to judge, I can trust the advice and wait to see if a new solution or new information or a new action comes to me.

And what all three of these sayings do for me is remind me of the circle of things I can control, all the things about myself that are in my power: my attitude, my actions, my ability to learn new skills, the things I choose to say and how I say them, the things I choose to keep to myself. When you think about it that way, that's a lot of power. I may not be powerful in the eyes of the world—but I *am* the most powerful person in that small, inner circle of my life.

· 2 ·
Your Self Is a Work in Progress

Ever since I was a little girl, people have told me I am "too sensitive." I complained when a breeze made me cold, while others thought it was still plenty warm. I was so scared by the flying monkeys in *The Wizard of Oz* that I hid behind my dad's big chair until the scene was over. If someone criticized me or disagreed with me, I would feel so hurt that I'd either run home crying or lash out with angry words. When I experienced something I really liked—a great book or a ride at the carnival or a beautiful sight—I'd get so excited I could hardly contain myself. When I would try to say something I felt deeply or do something I had never done before or meet new people, I'd get nervous and wind up shy, with my voice choked up or legs shaking, even if it didn't show on the outside.

To me, those reactions seemed normal and "just the way I was," but other people seemed to see them as evidence that I was weak or ridiculously emotional. Inside, I started to feel as though the way I experienced the world was somehow wrong, that I was supposed to hide the strong feelings I had, that I couldn't measure up or fit in, that I was too different, and that difference was a bad thing.

As I grew, I realized that while I sometimes felt negative emotions, like anger and sadness and fear, more strongly than others,

I also felt positive things strongly, like the joy of a sunset, amazement at a work of art, or the comfort of a cat's fur touching my skin. I started to see that I have higher highs and lower lows than a lot of other people do, and I started figuring out that I couldn't be like a lot of the other kids, who always seemed to me to be in crowds doing lots of activities. I didn't really like being in a crowd much—even though I sometimes felt awfully lonely on my own. I needed quiet times sitting by the lake or alone in my room listening to music or writing in my journal. I liked being with one or two friends at a time, not in a huge bunch. I thought that meant I was not interesting or appealing, that I should have a big group of friends but didn't, so there must be something wrong with me.

I learned ways to hide my sensitivity and to cope with it: I learned from my mom how to make small talk with strangers so I didn't worry so much about meeting new people; I learned to pretend that I was outgoing, to smile when I didn't feel like it; I learned to calm myself down when I got nervous so I could speak up when I had to, to purposely decide what feelings to let show on my face. It helped some, too, to read books and see movies like *Catcher in the Rye* and *Stand and Deliver* that showed other people who grappled with being different. I read dozens of biographies of interesting people (like Florence Nightingale), and discovered many of them had felt different as teenagers, too. But I still didn't really get away from the feeling of being "not quite right."

This feeling went on for years, into my twenties and thirties, into and out of my relationships, into and through the different jobs I had and the different places I lived. I carried that feeling along with me, deep inside.

Then something happened a few years ago. I was sitting in a coffee shop reading a magazine called the *Utne Reader*. As I paged through, I saw a headline for an article that asked, "Are You a Highly Sensitive Person?" And I thought to myself, Well, I guess so, everyone has told me I'm *too* sensitive since I was little. So I started reading.

What a revelation! According to the author, Elaine N. Aron, lots of people are just like me in that way. About 15 to 20 percent of the population, boys and girls and men and women of all races, have highly sensitive nervous systems. That's not a large percentage, but in populous countries like the U.S., it means millions of people. Here's how the author describes it:

> HSPs are born with a [highly receptive, highly sensitive nervous system] that makes them aware of all kinds of subtle messages from outside and inside. It's not that our eyes or ears are sharper. It's that we process more deeply the information we receive. We like to reflect . . . we are good with infants, animals, and plants— and in any situation in which it helps to notice subtle signs . . . . We also . . . [are] more easily overwhelmed by nonsubtle or strong stimulation: Noise. Visual clutter. Scratchy fabrics. "Funny" odors and food that's slightly "off" or tainted. Temperature extremes and all sorts of sudden changes. Emotionally evocative situations. Crowds. Strangers. And if we process information more deeply, we are going to dwell longer on the meaning of criticisms, rejection, betrayals, losses, and deaths . . . it is a neutral, normal trait, with advantages and disadvantages.

Aha! So, I wasn't so strange after all! I may not be like the majority of people (who I sometimes think of in my meaner moments as "undersensitive"), but I'm not a freak—at least, not in the bad sense (sometimes I think everyone is a freak in one or way or another). I'm not "deficient" or "weak" or overly emotional. Suddenly I was able to say not "I'm too sensitive," but simply "I'm sensitive."

I went right out to the library and found Aron's book, *The Highly Sensitive Person: How to Thrive When the World Overwhelms You,* and as I read, little things, little memories, began to click into place:

- My mother telling me that when I was a toddler, little more than a year old, I came to her as she was sitting on the couch in the living room, having the beginning of labor pains in her pregnancy with my little brother. She said I seemed to notice she wasn't feeling good, even though she was trying to hide it from me and my older brother, and I leaned against her leg, patting her comfortingly on the knee, as if I knew.

- How I had always loved the fairy tale "The Princess and the Pea," about how you could tell a true princess by the sensitive way she could perceive a single pea under the mattresses she slept on.

- The overwhelming feelings of intimidation I would get when I tried to speak in front of a group of people.

- The way friends had told me, in various ways, to "just get over it," impatient with how deeply I felt things and how long it took me, compared to them, to work through experiences.

- An Easter Sunday long ago when Dad and I both noticed a big lily bud on the table actually pop open as we watched, and what a big deal that was to us.

- How I sometimes seem to be the first in a group to detect subtle signals that things aren't going well or that there is trouble ahead.

So, at age 39, I took this big new step in learning to accept myself, in seeing that what I'd been told so many times was "wrong" with me wasn't wrong at all. It was just the body type and temperament I'd been given. Since then, I've worked hard to accept it, to figure out how to understand it myself, to help other people understand it, and to learn techniques for managing that aspect of myself. For example, I've learned that my strong feelings often need time to subside before

I can express them accurately and respectfully. So I practice waiting before speaking and sometimes ask friends and colleagues to postpone a discussion for a day to allow me time to process.

It's been a true joy to see more clearly what gifts and challenges I was given simply by being born as my sensitive self. I've also taken a closer look at how the things that have happened to me have affected who I am, and ultimately how I'm choosing to work on myself and make the best of myself that I can.

Do you see yourself as a highly sensitive person? If these characteristics don't describe you, maybe this information will help you interact with family members or friends you've considered "too sensitive." Whichever way you are, it can be really helpful to discover that there is not just one way to be!

Finding Out Who You Are

I was reading some more in Aron's book about highly sensitive people the other day and came across a funny metaphor. She suggests that when we think about ourselves, it's helpful to think about dogs. There are all kinds of dogs: big and small, multicolored and single colored, yippy and growling, pure breeds and mutts. Greyhounds are sensitive dogs who love to run and hunt; border collies are high-energy dogs that love to work hard and play hard with their humans; pit bulls are strong and protective by nature but can be easily trained to be fierce fighters. Greyhounds are very different from border collies, and both are very different from pit bulls, but they're all good dogs in their own ways. If you were a dog, what kind would you be?

It's worthwhile finding out how we're the same and different from others as we come to understand who we are and who we want to become. But we can also stop doing the kind of comparing that just makes us feel bad—like wanting to be a Doberman when you're really a poodle or Pomeranian at heart—and start focusing on ourselves as we are.

There are all kinds of self-discovery themes you can think about. I've already mentioned sensitivity. The basic themes are all part of being human, but each human has his own mix, her own place on the continuum, for example, from not very sensitive at all to highly sensitive. Another might be playfulness and seriousness. Another might be how changeable your moods are, from staying mostly even to having high highs and low lows.

One of the fundamental things we know about ourselves is whether we are male or female. At first glance, it might seem fairly obvious. But gender distinctions aren't necessarily easy for everyone; there are people who feel female inside despite being born male on the outside, and vice versa. Some find that rather than only being attracted to the opposite sex, they are attracted instead or also to their own. Hmmm, it's already not so simple, eh?

And within the broad categories of female and male, there are more continuums, more variations. Because even though as a group males or females tend to have a lot in common, each individual female or male expresses a unique combination of traits.

Traditionally, males tend to have certain characteristics in common: they are likely to be taller and physically stronger than females; many are interested in how things work; they may on average be more assertive and aggressive than women . . . that sort of thing. Some of these tendencies may feel natural, and others may be influenced by expectations in society. But any particular male is going to have his own unique characteristics and will share only some of those "typical" male traits. One male might be much more interested in working with children than with machines or technology or other "things." A different male might find that he loves exercising and building his muscles, but would rather act in plays than play football. Another might want to do all of these things.

It's the same with females. Females as a group often value caring about others, sometimes to the point that they don't care enough about themselves. They may enjoy talking with their friends a lot, about everything from fashion or physical appearance to relationships to the meaning of life. But any particular female is going to share only some of those "typical" female traits. One might be a person who is quite emotional but channels her feelings into competitive sports. Another might be very into relationships and caring for others, but may also value highly her independence, and prefer less talk and more action.

you get to be a sculptor of yourself; take the clay you were born with and shape it.

You might feel even more confused by gender expectations if you are gay, lesbian, or bisexual. Some people think that being a gay man makes you feminine, and being a lesbian woman makes you masculine. The truth is that your interests and traits are not dictated by your sexuality. Lots of factors contribute to the person you are, and sexual orientation is only one piece of the puzzle.

Each of us gets to choose what particular kind of man or woman we want to be, given the "raw materials" we start with. You get to be a sculptor of yourself: find out what kind of clay you were born with and into and then figure out how you want to shape it.

What's important is that you figure this stuff out for yourself, not dwelling only on the things other people expect you to be and not wasting a lot of time comparing yourself to others—or letting them compare you. You can learn some things from caring friends and family and teachers, but you need to do your own personal exploration, too. What are you really, deep inside? Do you feel things strongly and spend time emotionally "processing" events, or do you like to take action and see how it works out? Do you think things over in silence, or do you think the best when talking things out with a friend? Do you like to be alone when you get into a bad mood, or do you need to be with other people? Do you prefer having one or two close friends, or do you like to have different kinds of friends and do most things as a group?

There's no single right answer to questions like these; the answer that is true for *you* is the one that's right for you.

Your Inner Life

If it seems difficult to find out who you are, what you have been naturally given, try to think back to your childhood, when you were 9 or 10 or 11 years old. When I think back, I remember I loved reading, playing imaginative games, making up stories, watching cartoons, playing outside on the swing set or my bike, coloring, playing dress up, playing with the kitty.

You can also ask your parents or other adults who cared for you what you were like when you were little; they saw you a lot, and while they may put their own interpretations on what you were like, as mine did about being sensitive, they'll give you clues.

Another way is to read about all kinds of specific people to find out what they were like and how they lived. You can read autobiographies and biographies of all kinds of fascinating people: sports stars like Ty Cobb, Mia Hamm, and Venus Williams; musicians like John Lennon, Joni Mitchell, Macy Gray, and Justin Timberlake; artists like Frida Kahlo, Keith Haring, Christo, and Laurie Anderson; people who did things first, like Jackie Robinson, the first black major league baseball player, or Ellen Ochoa, the first Latina astronaut. You can use these books to find out what other people have been given and what they've done with it, and that can be a helpful perspective when you're learning to look at yourself and your own life and your future.

Another way is to find out about people in general, and see what parts fit for you. There are all kinds of personality tests and surveys you can look at. The Myers-Briggs Type Indicator® is one that helps you see if you're more of an extrovert or an introvert, if you're more deliberate in your choices or more spontaneous, and other traits like that. You can ask a librarian or school guidance counselor (they would probably be *thrilled* to have you ask for this) to help you find interest inventories you can take to find out what kinds of jobs you might be best at because they fit with who you are. And you can look at books about religion and philosophy and poetry that help you become skilled at figuring all this out, what some people call "self-examination."

The important point is that you truly undertake to find out about yourself intentionally, to find out for yourself what kind of personality traits and temperament and abilities are the "givens" in your life, the things that you need to accept and even embrace about yourself. After all, if you're going to sculpt yourself and your own life, you've got to know something about the kind of clay you've got to work with.

The Life around You

Besides the givens that are inside of you, there are givens on the outside as well, the circumstances of your birth and life. I was born into a certain kind of family, in a certain kind of town, at a certain moment of history—and so were you. As for myself, I was born the second child, first girl, in a family of six, in a middle-sized town called Sioux Falls, South Dakota, and grew up during the 1960s and 1970s. What about you?

- Where do you live? In a crowded city neighborhood or on a farm or in a small town? Surrounded by lots of different kinds of people or in an area where most people are the same race and religion?
- Have you been healthy all your life or have you had sickness or injuries to deal with?
- Do you have lots of interests and talents or just a few special ones?
- And what about your family? Are you growing up with two parents who live together, or two who live apart, or only one, or one parent and a step-parent, or grandparents, or a guardian, or a foster family, or in a group home?
- Are your parents or guardians healthy and happy or are they ill or troubled?
- Do they have jobs they like? Have they ever lost their jobs?
- Do they struggle to make ends meet or do they earn plenty of money?
- Are you an only child, or do you have siblings, step-siblings, or half-sisters and brothers? If you have siblings, are you the first child or middle or youngest? Are you an older brother or sister or a younger one?
- Did your parents or guardians read to you and play with you, or were they too busy to do that?
- Do you have lots of relatives you know and are close to, or are your relatives distant?

Probably there is no one who is more influential in your life than your parents or the people who have been most like parents to you. Whether that relationship has been mostly a good, close one or mostly a difficult, distant one or somewhere in between, the time and energy you have spent interacting together has a powerful shaping influence on you and your future relationships. Most people find that their relationship with their parents changes over the years as they themselves change. If you're lucky, and if both you and your parents are working on it and on yourselves, you'll gradually develop a more mature relationship that helps you move through your teens and twenties with love, understanding, encouragement—and hopefully some fun!

For me, it wasn't all that easy, and I can see now that both my parents and I played a part in that. I got rebellious, fought with my parents a lot, and broke their rules, and it took until I was in my twenties and thirties before we started to develop a good relationship. Somehow, as I got older and more mature, I was able to start seeing them not just as my mom and dad, but also as other people, people who were struggling to figure out who they were and what they should do, just as much as I was. And I got a little more tolerant, more patient, more accepting, less judgmental.

Now, in my forties, I can look back and see more clearly some of what they and my other life circumstances gave me. Mom taught me, through her swing into the 1970s feminist movement (which at times seemed pretty weird and annoying), to be a happily random housekeeper, to not be a slave to fashion, to feel free to view reading or playing the piano as more important than chores. Dad, who was highly sensitive like me, taught me the joys of reading and thinking and joking. My siblings helped me learn about being there for each other, about how to get along and how to make up again after a fight, and about how different people can wind up with really different views of the same event.

I can see now, looking back, that many of the circumstances of my life have contributed to both my uniqueness and my commonalities with others. My growing up in the sixties and seventies—when young people were fighting for civil rights and against the war in Vietnam—made me take it for granted that teenagers could have important ideas and do important things, like vote and protest and try to change the world for the better. I was also lucky enough to spend a year in England with my family when I was in sixth grade. That experience introduced me to the thrills and fears of seeing brand-new landscapes, of hearing people speak with different accents and in different languages, and of how different cultures can sometimes make a person feel like a complete stranger or more at home than ever before. No matter what your background is, your circumstances have made you the unique person you are.

Some people really want to separate themselves from their roots: their families, their histories, their cultures, and so on. But for me, it's important to remember that all my experiences, good and difficult, have contributed to who I am and to making me unique, just as your life circumstances and family have for you. And because these memories and family and experiences are all woven into who we are, they stay with us throughout our lives, even if our understandings of them change over time. It's like a kaleidoscope: the memories and family and experiences are all the bits of multi-colored glass inside of it, and when you turn the end of the kaleidoscope as you grow and change, you see different patterns.

Being Different

I must admit, there are still times when being unique doesn't feel like such a great thing. Sometimes what I really want is to belong, to feel like part of something. So I continue to ponder about people, about being unique and about being similar, about others and about myself.

I've always been curious about people in general, and I've also felt pushed into exploring who I am, because I kept running up against this notion that I wasn't like everyone else. When I was little, I liked fairy tales when everyone else was reading the popular new book series. I had more fun playing with my cat than with dolls or other toys. When I was older, people at high school seemed to think

I was too serious, that I spent too much time thinking and not enough just having fun. For a long time that feeling of being different wasn't a good one; it made me feel alone and isolated, alienated and strange.

Part of that, it turns out, was just an illusion. "Everyone else" felt different, too. One of the funniest, strangest events of my life was attending my 10-year high school reunion. (This was the whole school's reunion, not just the students from the alternative school.) I went with Lori, who had been my best friend at the Compass School, and reconnected with some women who had been our good friends in junior high. Together we sat at a table and were stunned by all the changes in people: the star football player who had been so cute wasn't so much anymore; the perky cheerleader who we thought was "snotty" had gotten rather motherly looking and really friendly; men who had been popular boys who never gave us a second look back then stopped by our table and talked with us as if we were interesting people; and we talked with people who had never been close friends, but who now seemed to share more in common with us than we'd ever imagined. And as we talked about high school and our lives since then, we all found out that each of us had gone through a lot of the same feelings: fears and worries about being good enough, cool enough, smart enough, pretty or handsome enough, and had worried especially about being different. What a joke! If everyone is different, does that make us all the same in our "differentness"?

The most interesting idea I took away from that reunion was how each of us had been affected—mostly negatively—by our perceptions of the various groups in high school. We saw the cliques as the popular kids, the jocks, the druggies, the nerds. (Today I also hear terms like "ghetto" and "preps.") The whole idea of needing to fit in somewhere—to belong, to be like everyone else in a certain group—made a lot of us feel as if we didn't fit *anywhere*. But when we were able to talk to one another as individuals ten years later, the groups didn't seem as important anymore. In fact, we realized that while it used to seem as if the groups existed on their own to judge whether we were worthy to fit in, we actually had the power (there's that word again) to be with the people we were interested in. (If you want a good illustration of what I mean, and a fun look at hardcore '80s fashion, watch the movie *The Breakfast Club*.)

One of the tricky things I've been learning as I get older is when to focus on seeing myself as a unique and different individual and when to focus on the ways I am (or want to be) similar to a larger group. Because I, like everyone else, am both a member of many groups and a unique individual at the same time, all the time. No wonder we feel so weird sometimes.

So now, I feel as though much of the time I can choose to fit in or not to (or choose simply to accept that I'm different from the current group). Think of it this way: It's important to fit in when the group or the group's best interest is the most important thing. For me, this idea is most relevant when I'm at work. In our organization there are many project teams and meetings of small groups that have to get things accomplished to reach mutual goals. In order to work well together, we each have to bring our own unique strengths and abilities to the table, but most important, we have to be able to get along, to speak the same language, to follow the same processes. If each of us held up our individuality and our own unique ways constantly, we'd likely spend all our time arguing and disagreeing about how and what to do and we'd accomplish nothing.

This is the same kind of truth you learn when you do a ropes course, or play lacrosse, or play in an orchestra, or any other kind of activity where the whole is greater than the sum of the parts. No matter how different you are from the other people there, you have to find a way to work together or you won't get the whole team across the ropes, or the ball into the net, or the notes in sync.

So you pull together, and you start thinking more of the team than of just yourself and your own ideas . . . and it works. You find you can be or become confident in yourself and respected for your individuality, but still set aside your ego enough to concentrate on being a team member.

Sometimes not fitting in is unintentional on your part, and that can feel hurtful and lonely. For example, you can wind up not fitting in to any groups in high school because your looks and clothes are different. That might be because you are mixed race when most everyone else is either white or black; it might be because your family can't afford (or doesn't care about) trendy fashions in clothing; or it might be because you wear a brace for scoliosis or orthodontic headgear for your teeth and jaws. In these cases, you still have choices: You can be angry or sad about not fitting in, or you can decide whether or not your values are different from the values of the others in the group; you can find cool clothes at a thrift store, or try to start a new trend by doing something really unusual, like wearing one of your grandma's or grandpa's suits to school; you can do something dramatic, like color your hair, to draw attention to that part of your appearance, or work on being a good friend and having a positive attitude so that people get to know *you* instead of just what you look like.

sometimes being different is the best thing to do.

At other times, being different is more of a choice. For example, you may choose in an art class to do a painting unlike anyone else's; maybe yours is on a T-shirt or a bedsheet instead of on a canvas; maybe yours is filled with neon colors when everyone else is using natural colors. You may choose to write and sing songs that no one else likes, but that are your very own, because that is the music that is inside of you, even if it's too angry sounding and the bass is too loud for other people's taste. It's a matter of following your own inclination and inspiration, something you can learn to do more and more as you grow. One of the little things I choose to do that makes me different from a lot of people my age is that I don't dress up for work. It's more important to me, as long as I'm clean and neat, to wear clothes that are comfortable instead of fancy suits that say "money" and "power," and shoes that are good for my feet instead of high heels that say "feminine" and "fashionable." Lucky for me, I have a boss who, even though she is pretty stylish, is a lot more concerned with the quality of my thinking and my work than with the appearance of my clothes!

There are also times when being different is the best thing to do. Sometimes it's even noble. My nephew, Thor, told me of a situation like that recently, from a time when he and his family were living in Spain (his step-dad's job took them there). In Spain, people can buy wine, beer, and hard cider (which also contains alcohol) at age 16. He had gone with some friends from the high school to have a picnic, and when they stopped at the store to buy food, some of the kids also bought wine and cider. Because of his own beliefs about not drinking as a teenager, he took the risk of being different and told his friends when they offered him some that he didn't drink alcohol. He didn't criticize them for doing it; he simply stated his own choice. And his friends just said, "Oh, that's cool, okay," and they all went on with their picnic. It was a small thing, just making one remark, but it was an important difference to state.

History shows us lots of examples of people choosing to be different, such as choosing to stand up for beliefs that are not the popular ones. For my parents' generation, some of the most admirable people like that were acting before and during the Second World War, when the Nazis, under Adolf Hitler, were systematically persecuting and killing Jews, Catholics, Gypsies, people who were gay, and people with disabilities. Millions were killed in Poland alone. (You can read *The Diary of a Young Girl* by Anne Frank or watch the movie *Schindler's List* for true stories of heroism in these circumstances.) A majority of the German people went along with the "racial cleansing" plans, and some even helped by turning in their friends and neighbors; others disagreed but were too afraid to speak out or do anything to try to stop it. There were, however, women and men throughout Poland, Germany, and elsewhere in Europe who expressed their differences by taking great risks, speaking out and sometimes being killed for their convictions, hiding threatened families in their attics and cellars, and operating underground escape routes. Their being different, their not fitting in, shows us human beings at their best.

For my friends and me in the 1960s and 1970s, many of our heroes were also those who chose to be different. At a time when blacks were considered second-class citizens and thus unfit to eat with whites or ride in the fronts of buses, we admired Rosa Parks, an African American who quietly sat in the front of a bus and thereby took the Civil Rights movement a big step forward. We admired Gandhi and Martin Luther King, Jr., for being nonviolent but still refusing to back down during volatile, turbulent times. And we admired other teenagers and twenty-somethings who were willing to differ from the many supporters of the Vietnam War by speaking out against it, holding sit-ins and other protests, and bringing to the world through their new and different music the ideas of peace, joy, and love.

Who is being a hero or a heroine now by being different? You may admire generous celebrities or political leaders who show integrity; on the other hand, you might find heroes in everyday life. Whom do you respect for being different? Is it your friend at school who refuses to buy a car and instead rides his bike everywhere because he thinks we depend too much on foreign oil? Is it your friend's parents who homeschool their kids so they can teach the values they believe are most important? Is it the classmate who wouldn't go along with the other kids in the cafeteria in making fun of a new student but instead spoke out and invited that new student to sit with her? Is it the boy who, in the midst of the noise and movement of the school, bows his head and offers a prayer of thanks before eating his lunch?

I'm Done Apologizing for Being Different

As I said a little while ago, I'm still learning about when to stand up for my differences and when to just accept them, and sometimes even when to hide them for a while. It's not an easy thing to learn, because every circumstance or situation I encounter seems to require new kinds of choices. Just this year I've been working a lot on being able to say who I am and what I like without apologizing for my taste in TV, movies, clothes, books, and so on. I'm getting better at accepting what I've been given and what my life circumstances have been, not trying to be someone else or someone else's idea of who I should be. I keep on choosing who I want to become.

I haven't always had the confidence to do that, or even realized that I needed to develop that part of myself. During the early 1990s, I had a big "Aha!" moment about accepting who I am and choosing who I want to become. I was married then to an artist; his artwork included taking and developing moody, atmospheric black-and-white photographs of landscapes, and then building wooden models of houses and temples to apply the photographs to—a kind of photographic sculpture. I was working as a freelance editor and writer, but not enjoying it much; it seemed a lot more interesting to focus our lives on my husband's obviously fascinating artwork. Most of our friends were his artist and museum friends, and I thought that was a fun crowd to hang around with.

One Saturday evening, we were invited to an artist party. There was going to be a bonfire in the backyard, where anyone who wanted to could burn their old yucky attempts at painting or writing or whatever other art they were doing. We arrived and my husband got pulled into a discussion with some other photographers, so I headed over to the food and drink before going out to see what was burning on the fire. While I was filling my plate, a really interesting-looking man came over to talk with me. He introduced himself and then asked about me. I started to say that I was married to an artist and that I came to the party with him and what his artwork was like. Then that interesting man got a funny look on his face and interrupted me. "I didn't ask about who your husband is," he said, "I asked about *you.*"

Oops.

That was the aha moment, one that I thought about a lot over the next days and weeks. How could I have gotten so far away from my own interests that when someone asked me about myself, I could only talk about someone else?

What I did next was pretty simple, looking back on it, but it was difficult at the time. I started trying new things, doing some of what I thought I might like, just as my husband did, so that I had my own stuff to talk about. I began borrowing new books from the library, volunteering to spend time with teenagers who were in a nearby juvenile detention center, and taking Tai Chi classes. I started seeing a counselor to help me understand more about my family and my place in it. I found a new job, at a magazine for wildlife artists, that combined my interest in art and animals with my love of reading, writing, and editing. I started expanding and broadening my horizons, spending time with a couple of new friends, and working at incorporating all these new things into my identity.

I decided to *claim* my own interests, my own self, as my friend, Liane, used to call it.

Nowadays, I comfortably say that I don't watch much TV without apologizing for the reason: I simply can't bear to watch the stupid commercials, and I don't have a system that lets me weed them out. When I meet people's pets, I act like a sentimental fool without worrying about what people think of me, because I accept and embrace my love of animals as an important part of who I am. And I visit a counselor once in a while, when life gets really tough and I need some help figuring out the new challenges that have come along, because I know that asking for help doesn't mean I'm weak; it means I'm committed to finding out more about myself, about other people, and about life.

I remember fondly when I was a little kid that my younger brother, Steve, had a book of riddles. He used to drive the rest of us kids crazy asking those riddles all the time and then laughing hysterically at the answers. The one I liked best went like this: "What is the biggest room in the world?" And the answer was, "Room for improvement." I still like that. It reminds me that as long as I live, I can keep on becoming myself by the ways I learn and grow.

· 3 ·
Body and Mind
Work Best
Together

Another of my favorite sayings refers to an old story from Asia. I think it's both true and funny, and it applies to all kinds of situations. The phrase is BE A SMART MONKEY.

The story as I've heard it goes like this: In small villages in Asia, the local people would sometimes catch monkeys, either to eat or to keep as pets. By observing how monkeys behaved in the wild, they came up with a clever trap. They would take a large gourd, hollowed out and dried, and make a hole just large enough for a monkey to reach into it with its paw. Then they would put rice inside of it, hide out near the gourd where monkeys would come, and wait.

When a hungry monkey would smell the rice, it would come to the gourd, reach in its paw, and grab a handful. But when it tried to pull out the rice, the monkey would discover that while the hole was big enough to put its empty paw inside, the hole wasn't big enough for pulling its rice-filled fist back out.

Imagine that monkey. It sees the villagers coming and it's frightened. But it's also hungry and wants the rice. The answer to the monkey's dilemma seems simple to us: Set aside your hunger, let go of the rice, pull out your paw, and run away. But that answer does not occur to most monkeys. The trap works because the monkey can't let go of what it wants, and won't see that the way it is grasping and holding on to the food is the source of its problem. It is unable to see that the short-term gratification of its hunger (holding on to the rice) is getting in the way of its long-term satisfaction (freedom). Its body and brain are not working well together. It cannot change its mind about how important the rice is in comparison with its life. It is not being a smart monkey.

Situations like this can happen to us humans, too, and often in connection to the things our body wants. We might keep eating things that taste good even when we know they aren't good for us or will give us heartburn or indigestion. We might drink too much or experiment with drugs or start smoking, because the initial physical sensations are pleasant or at least interesting, and we choose not to believe all the information we've heard about the bad effects. We might stay in a relationship with someone who is not a good friend to us because we fear being alone, or because we like the sense of togetherness, or because we think our love can help that person mend.

The answer for us, too, is to be smart monkeys. To let go when it's best for us, to learn to re-evaluate the things we thought we wanted or craved, to use our minds to help us figure out a balance that will lead to our long-term happiness, to look beyond the surface pleasures of our bodies to the deeper good of them.

What I mean by "be a smart monkey" is that deep down, and sometimes not so deep, we have instincts, natural ways of behaving that aren't always conscious, just like monkeys and other animals. We may have gone beyond a lot of other animals in our ability to think and reason and remember and laugh, but we haven't lost our animal nature; we've simply added those other abilities "on top," so to speak. We are all born with physical bodies, and we use our physical senses in every moment of our daily lives to bring us the information we need to avoid danger and meet our basic needs for food and drink, for shelter, for touching and being touched. We are body and mind together in one being. All that "animal stuff" is still in us, and we use it all the time, often unconsciously. We respond, for example, to other people's body language even more than to their words, at times. We find, if we try to be aware of it, that our bodily states of hunger, arousal, or tiredness influence our moods and behaviors quite dramatically. When I'm trying to understand what's going on in relationships, in groups of friends, in classrooms, on teams, in offices, in politics, in crowds, and most of all in myself, I try to be aware of my body's messages and bring my mind to the question of what I'm feeling and doing—and together, my body and mind bring me a clearer, more accurate picture of what's real and what's important.

Following the Rules, Making the Rules

When you're young, adults give you lots of rules about your body, don't they? Rules about sex, rules about food, rules about drink. I remember not liking those rules sometimes, not understanding them sometimes, and often finding them contradictory and confusing. Why shouldn't I eat three ice-cream bars in a row if they taste good? Why shouldn't I go down the hill on my bike as fast as I can? Why shouldn't I let myself have all the strong sensations of sexual activity? If one beer gives me a good feeling of relaxation and excitement, why shouldn't two or three beers make me feel even better?

It's all very confusing—there seem to be rules your parents give you, different ones you get from your friends, and still different ones from movies and TV and magazines and advertisements. Some rules are meant to protect and help you, some seem meant just to control you or manipulate you. One set of rules often conflicts with another. For example, on the one hand, there are social rules about how important it is to be sexually attractive, and on the other hand, religious or family rules about not acting on your sexual impulses. (And by the way, how can it be cool for a guy to have sex, but having sex makes a girl a so-called "slut," when scientists say it's a natural thing for both males and females!)

After making a lot of mistakes in judgment about following or not following certain rules—falling off my bike at the bottom of a steep hill because I was going faster than I could handle; later letting relationships get physical before I knew the other person well enough to know if there was true caring between us; sometimes drinking so much that I got dizzy and sick and acted stupid—after a lot of mistakes and quite a few years, I understand now that the best rules were there to give me time to be safe, to wait for my brain function to catch up with my body changes, to help me begin to make decisions about what I did with and put into my body rather than simply follow my physical impulses.

For example, if I'm feeling physically attracted to someone, the rule of waiting can usually help me make a good decision about how to act. By saying "not now" to myself, I give myself time to think about who or what is arousing me and what kind of choice I want to make. Is this someone I really want to get close to? Is this a good person as well as a person I find attractive? Am I better off just enjoying the feelings of arousal but dealing with them on my own (after all, I know lots of ways to make my body feel good)? Am I particularly lonely or vulnerable right now and perhaps looking for some reassurance that I'm desirable, pretty, interesting, whatever? I know I have to be in charge of my own protection against pregnancy and diseases; do I have with me what I need?

It would have helped me, though, when I was younger, if the rules had been explained better, so that I could understand those reasons of safety and the decision making behind them. I vaguely remember hearing that you should wait, at least until you're older if not until you're married, but I don't remember hearing convincing reasons why! What I know now is that sex without deep love, caring, and respect is empty and sometimes harmful to my spirit; that adding sex to a young relationship complicates it in unexpected ways; and that the potential physical consequences of disease and pregnancy are real and dangerous.

Now that I'm older, and have experienced a lot of mistakes as well as successes in using my mind and spirit in dealing with my body (and at times with other people's bodies), I've formulated my own rules, in my own words, in forms that I can understand, remember, and use. These work for me, and I can remember them because they are my own.

Mind and Body Rule #1: Don't Forget to Breathe This is an odd one, perhaps. You might think, "How could I ever forget to breathe?" But when humans get busy, nervous, scared, excited, or stressed out, one of the ways our bodies draw our attention to that fact is by starting to breathe quickly and shallowly.

When you study yoga, Tai Chi, and other Eastern practices that combine the spiritual, the mental, and the physical, you learn that breath is the bridge between body and mind; one of the most calming and centering activities you can do is the very simple one of breathing slowly and deeply. You can do it while sitting quietly and meditating or just relaxing (try it right now by closing your eyes and breathing in through your nose for four steady beats and out your mouth for six; it can help to get into an "alligator pose" on your belly with your hands crossed under your chin, elbows pointing straight out on either side). You can also do the exhale, in times of more need, through a little private screaming in the car or your bedroom when no one else is around. (Yep, I do that sometimes; it's called scream therapy.) You can practice breathing through an aerobic exercise like running, hiking, swimming, or rollerblading. And you can do it through singing.

Any of these activities will help you adjust your breathing to become deeper and more deliberate. And I've discovered for myself that this kind of breathing has a direct and almost immediate effect on my mind and body—both relax, both become more in tune, and no matter what the situation, I'm better prepared to handle it. I feel whole within myself, and in control of my body and emotions rather than being controlled by them.

Mind and Body Rule #2: Explore It, Revel in It, Protect It

Knowing your body helps you figure out when and how to trust your instincts, timing, and wisdom about when to act and when to wait. It gives you clues to what's happening and what you might need or want to do about it. This applies to relationships, sports, dance, sleep, eating, and more. It is the animal part of us—an important part—and a part we need to care for if we want it to care for us.

Your mind gets all kinds of information from your body. You know you are attracted to someone when you notice, for example, that you are sitting or standing a little straighter, leaning toward the person, or lifting your hand to stroke your own hair. I learn something potentially important when I find myself in a difficult meeting with someone, and I notice that I have folded my arms across my chest in a protective gesture and that my stomach muscles are tightening—both signs of fear. I discover I have more endurance than I realized when my energy kicks in from intense exercise, and I feel as if I could hike or bike or dance for hours.

In all three cases, my body is giving clues to my mind. In the first case, clues about a possible relationship. In the second, clues about possible danger. And in the third, about the thrill of what our bodies can do when we don't "psych ourselves out." When you take the time to get to know your body well and over time become aware of the signals it gives you through all your senses, you can more easily sort out mentally whether the clues your body is giving you are good ones to act on. The attraction may be to someone who is good looking but perhaps does not share your values or have integrity. The fear may be more about your own nervousness than about the other person actually being dangerous. And it's not a good idea to exercise until you drop, but maybe you can go just a little bit further than you first expected.

The thing to do is to find ways both to enjoy your body and to protect it. We need to feed our bodies with nutritious food and plenty of water, to use our bodies physically, through exercise, through sports, maybe through touching ourselves or others, so that we can experience that amazing sense of oneness between body and mind that is our truest experience of human life. And we need to be careful about putting alcohol and other drugs into our bodies, because they can have serious effects on both our body and mind.

I'm now very purposeful about doing stretches each morning and trying to make time every week for exercise. I like to try new things through cheap community education classes, like yoga or African dance or martial arts, to find out what kinds of movements work with my natural strengths and make me feel good. When I'm really stressed, I like to arrange for a full-body massage, when I can afford it—nothing helps me let go of angst like a good revel in the feeling of having my body fully relaxed.

When I'm confused or afraid or angry, I try to notice my body. I concentrate on it, try to see it from inside and outside, and then stop and think about what I've noticed. I check to see where my muscles are tensed or relaxed, whether my body is hungry or thirsty or tired. And I take the answers into account as I figure out what the situation is, what my part in it is, and what I might want to do about it.

Mind and Body Rule #3: Try to Be a Good Animal No matter
how intelligent we are, how skilled at making things and moving
things around the globe, how complicated our thinking and our relationships, we remain human animals. Some might find that an
irritating thought, as if I'm putting down humans. But I don't mean
to. I just think it is a perspective that helps us to have the right kind
of humility and avoid the worst kinds of egotism. My favorite short
version of this idea is from a mystery novel by P. D. James called
Death in Holy Orders: "Maybe we'd do better if we tried to behave
more like good animals and less like gods."

I believe this quote reminds us of one of the bits of knowledge we
forget as we grow up and become "civilized." Through technology
and our separation from the natural world, and maybe too much
emphasis on our brains, we can wind up too focused on controlling
and dominating our world. We can lose some of the conscious connection to our bodies that animals have (they have to be more in
tune with their bodies and environments in order to survive) and
that we had so naturally as children. I've found, though, that I can
recapture it if I make a point of using and being aware of my body.

Perhaps the most dramatic way I've become aware again of my
animal qualities is through my experiences of wilderness camping.
I occasionally leave behind the trappings of cars and jobs and offices
and streets and artificial lights and spend a week or two traveling
only on my own two feet, carrying my food and drink with me, and
being physical outdoors for most of the day. Within a few days I
find myself much more aware of the feelings of my body, the sounds
of other creatures and the wind and my own footsteps, the drifting
scents in the air, changes in temperature. I slip quickly into a natural
rhythm of waking with the sun and going to sleep shortly after night-
fall. And I begin to experience myself in a more settled, comfortable,
integrated way; there doesn't seem to be such a complicated rela-

tionship between my thoughts and my body; they begin to work more easily as one.

And so, for at least a little while, I let go of my ambitions, my worries, my concerns about making it and succeeding and winning and controlling my life . . . and I just live. I know completely that I belong in the world, just as much as each deer or jackrabbit or lizard I encounter. And, for at least a little while after I return to my life in the city, I hold on to the feeling of wholeness and relatedness to the world that I have out there, and my desire is to live within nature as a part of it, rather than to live separately from it or to dominate it.

"maybe we'd do better if we tried to behave more like good animals and less like gods."

Of course, I can't always take off for the wilderness when I need a mental-health day (or week!). Sometimes I can't afford it financially; sometimes my job and family obligations and the classes I'm taking don't let me leave; sometimes I'm just too busy to get away. At those times, I try to come up with miniature getaways that help me achieve some of the same thoughts and feelings on a smaller scale.

Sometimes I go out the door into the open air, choose a direction, and just start walking. I might head for the nearest park or the river, or I might just walk in the neighborhood. I try to notice all things natural: the temperature of the air, whether it's dry or wet, how it feels on my skin; the sounds of pigeons or seagulls or squirrels or wind; the flowers in the neighborhood garden; the way the light falls in changing patterns on the sidewalk.

Sometimes I do another sort of getaway: I try to experience something new. It might be by getting on the bus and riding through a part of town I haven't been in before; it might be attending some sort of free event (a dog show or a presentation at a history center or a new exhibit at the modern art museum on free day); it might be a visit to the nearest park, where I can try out the kids' swings or try to count how many different kinds of bushes and trees are planted there. No matter what it is, if I concentrate on observing all the new and unfamiliar sights, sounds, and smells, I quickly begin to feel as if I'm on a mini-vacation. My mind turns off from the routine, from the worries and the troubles and the work to be done, and joins with my body as it moves through the new experience, to bring me new thoughts and feelings and ideas.

In my daily life, I can try to be a good animal: to take care of my body and mind, to use them together to live the best life I can. When I'm confused or frustrated or stressed, I can turn to the natural world and to my body's needs and feelings for clues. And when I can't get away and need some immediate relief, some way of pulling together my body and mind into a whole, I can try to be a smart monkey by letting go of whatever it is I seem to be grasping on to. And just breathe.

Yeah, but Let's Get Back to Sex!

I know, it's one of my favorite topics, too . . . but certainly not a simple one. There are lots of complications around sexuality in human society— to express our sexual feelings we choose special clothes, apply cosmetics, shave, perfume ourselves, dance; we have rules about it set by religious leaders and political leaders and our parents and our friends; there are fads and fashions about it, books about how to do it and how not to do it. It is rooted, though, in instinctive urges to mate and to experience good physical sensations, urges we share with virtually every other animal on the planet, urges that begin for us as humans with the body changes that take us from childhood into adolescence.

I remember in my teens when my body started to feel like someone's science experiment: changes to my shape, my skin, my level of hairiness, even. I confess, it sort of freaked me out for quite a while. I didn't know who I was anymore; I didn't feel like my old self, and I didn't know who my new self was supposed to be. I started having those "special feelings" they hinted at in the embarrassing booklets on puberty that our parents or teachers gave us. And those hormone-surge feelings were so strong and confusing—and sometimes downright inconvenient!

Now, in my forties, I can look back and not be embarrassed, and sometimes even laugh a little about it all, but I can also remember (as most people can, if they try) what it was like when I was first learning to feel it and deal with it. I remember feeling sure at 12 and 13 and 14 that my body was all wrong, it didn't look right; I had knobby knees and pointy elbows and my nose was getting bigger and I was too skinny and suddenly I had breasts and boys would look at them. A friend of mine remembers that when she wanted to start shaving under her arms, her mom told her the hair would grow back thicker and darker. She tried it anyway, and then panicked, thinking that her mom would make her stop and she'd end up with black, coarse fur in her armpits. A male friend remembers that his feet reached their adult size about a year before his body caught up with them. Another was bothered by being very short throughout high school and then relieved when he sprouted to six feet at age 19. My brother, Steve, assures me that both boys and girls experienced similar embarrassed or curious feelings in the shower at school after gym class, seeing others developing faster or slower than ourselves.

As I got a little older, at 15 and 16, I started experiencing times when it felt more important than anything else to find out whether I was physically attractive. I also began having vague ideas when kissing or cuddling with a date that there would soon come a time when I would want to do more. (I'll tell you a story about that later, about the feelings I had, what I knew or thought I knew, the mistakes I made, and what I did about it.)

For now, though, I'm thinking a lot more about what I *didn't* know. When I talked to some of my friends while I was writing this book, I found out that, like me, almost every one of them had pretended when they were a teenager that they knew a lot more about their bodies and sexuality than they really did.

So I came up with two things that I wish someone had told me about sex when I was a teenager, things I wound up finding out for myself the hard way, things that would've helped me get that mind-and-body-together perspective a little sooner. I think they would've saved me from a lot of confusion and a few mistakes, too.

When you feel confused, you need more information. The hormones that start invading our bloodstreams as bodies begin to change from children's bodies to adult male and female bodies throw the whole body-and-mind equation out of whack. We start getting a lot of new messages from our bodies, and since our brains are also still forming and changing, it's like our brains can't catch up fast enough.

When I was teenager, I did get some basic anatomy information in health class, and some advice to just not "do it." But that sure wasn't enough to help me make good choices. I didn't get a lot of communication about it from my family, either; my parents were pretty uncomfortable discussing any of the workings of the human body, let alone the sexual ones. My mom did give me the book *Our Bodies, Ourselves* when I was about 16, though, and that helped me quite a bit to understand more about the female body. It's strange to look back now and remember that at the time, the book was considered radical and was banned in libraries and schools around the country. Why? Because it gave girls and women information about their own bodies. Nowadays, that kind of information and more is much more readily available to young people, which I think is a very good thing.

I wish I'd had the smarts back then to realize that there was a lot I needed to learn about both female and male bodies, about discussing sex and about contraception and disease prevention, and especially about the emotional and psychological aspects of the whole range of sexual activities.

Knowing both genders' body stuff (and I'm talking about data here, not mutual exploration ☺) can help you make good choices and be understanding; it can help you have a more satisfying and healthy sexual life as an adult; and it can help you learn to be accepting of differences and appreciative of the uniqueness that each of us brings to each interaction we share. For example, did you know that both males and females have testosterone *and* estrogen hormones in their systems, just in different amounts and proportions? Did you know that both males and females have hormonal cycles, with females having monthly cycles and males having daily cycles?

You have to admit, this could be some pretty interesting homework, eh? So think of these three sources of information to study: accurate books and Web sites; honest, caring, trustworthy adults; and your growing knowledge of your own body (not necessarily in that order).

I'm a bookish sort of person, so I always start with books when I want and need information. If you want ideas, there are some good ones listed at the back of this book. If you prefer the Internet for information hunting, there's a lot out there, but you have to use more caution; Web sites don't necessarily go through the same kinds of fact-checking for accuracy that most books do. And while some of the sites out there include some (or even a lot of) arousing words and pictures, surfing porn sites doesn't really add to your knowledge; in fact, it can give you some very wrong ideas about the ways people deserve to be treated. You'll find you're better off looking at reputable sites like www.goaskalice.com or www.canadian-health-network.ca.

If you and at least one of your parents have a strong, close relationship, that's one of the best places to go for information; you can ask the real questions you have in safety and in private. Whether that's true for you or not, you can also look elsewhere for an honest, caring adult to talk with, whether that's a friend's parent, or your clergy person, or your school counselor, or your favorite teacher. The best of these adults will blend their factual answers with their caring for and knowledge of you as a unique person, and that will make their advice and counsel more valuable.

Finally, don't neglect to get to know your own body. "Masturbation" is the term used in health classes sometimes, but I find that word sounds awfully technical for something as natural and pleasant as touching yourself. It's a great way to learn about the kinds of touch that feel good to you, and it's also a great way to deal with feelings of arousal that you've decided not to act on with another person. In some cases, young people have been taught by their parents or by their religion that touching themselves could lead to things like acne or even blindness; thank goodness scientists have proven these ideas are completely untrue.

It was my friend, Christine, who helped me get past that old idea. She and I met during our first year in college, and when I turned 18, we got our very first apartment together. One day I came home from classes and didn't think she was home. I wound up walking in on her touching herself in her bedroom. (Okay, talk about life freaking me out!) A little later she joined me out in the living room, but she wasn't nearly as embarrassed as I was. She was so matter-of-fact that soon we were able to talk about masturbating and orgasms, and she even told me about methods she liked best. Well, that was all news to me. I felt sort of funny about it, but I did start experimenting with touching my own body in different ways, and I gained a lot of new knowledge from that.

Pretending you know more than you do doesn't help.

I remember quite vividly the first time I had sexual intercourse. (I gotta tell you, this feels kind of weird and vulnerable to write about my experiences with sex so honestly and matter-of-factly, but I want you to hear about real experiences, not just secondhand ones or made-up ones about someone who only does the right things and doesn't make any mistakes.) It wasn't really planned, at least on my part. I was in high school and dating a guy who was in college. After we'd gone out to a play, he invited me to his dorm room. We started out kissing, and then his hands started moving over my body. I was nervous and unsure, but I was also amazed at the sensations, thinking, "Nothing anyone has told me prepared me for this!" I didn't know how good it could feel, or how hard it would be to stop once started, or how I wouldn't want to stop, or how to talk about the situation, either.

But I was uncomfortable enough with how fast things were moving that I might have stopped it—except that the guy said something flattering to me about doing it well, and then I didn't want to admit that I'd never done it before! I didn't want him to think I was foolish or immature. So I kept my mouth shut and pretended that I was more experienced than I was. I remember him walking me home that evening, and after he left I stood by the gate in our backyard fence, feeling as if the experience had changed me, and I looked forward to seeing him again and talking about it.

Except he didn't call the next day, or the next, or the next, and in those days, it was still pretty unusual for a girl to call a guy. And as the days went by and I felt worse and worse, I wished I hadn't pretended; I wished I'd been honest—about my lack of experience, about my doubts and fears, about my feelings and values.

Now I realize that that honesty would have set the stage for either a relationship of respect, for ourselves and each other, or it would have shown me that a relationship with him wasn't the right thing for me. We could have talked about whether "going all the way" was the right thing to do, about contraception if we decided to go ahead, and we could have helped each other through the maze of changes we were going through in our bodies, our minds, and our behaviors.

That was a long time ago now, but I guess you can tell from the fact that I remember it so well that it was a significant event in my life, and one I wish I'd known how to handle with my mind as well as my body. These days, I'm adjusting to some new changes in my body, changes that have to do with aging. It's harder to stay slender, I get tired more easily, I've got crinkly lines around my eyes, and sometimes when I ask my body to stretch or move in a certain way, it says no. But along with the changes over time, my body and mind continue to work together and interact, each influencing the other. What's remarkable to me now is how it seems that I can use my body, with its hungers, urges, and sensations, as a kind of early alert system; how I can learn about my emotions and thoughts from what my body tells me, and how I can then bring my mind in on my physical feelings and urges and modify them, choose which ones to act on.

· 4 ·
Relationships with Others Depend on Your Relationship with Yourself

I went to Lakewood Cemetery the other day, the most
beautiful cemetery I've ever seen, here in Minneapolis. It has winding roads, hills, trees, old statues and gravestones, a lake surrounded
by pink flowering trees, and hillsides that in the early summer are
populated with families of ducks and geese. The weather was sweet
and warm and sunny, the air fresh and clean after recent rains.

I was going to meet my older brother, Todd, to visit our grandparents' graves on Memorial Day weekend and clean the overgrown
grass from them and talk a bit about our lives and this book. Todd
and I haven't always gotten along well; we're very different from
one another in our politics and our spirituality and our ways of life.
But he's been reaching out to me since I broke up with my boyfriend
of four years, and he called to suggest getting together. I'm purposely trying to say yes to invitations these days, even though part
of me just wants to crawl into a hole some days and stay there with
my hurt and anger and sadness, so I agreed to meet him.

I'd been to this cemetery a number of times before, sometimes alone, sometimes with my ex-husband before we got divorced. I always feel soothed by its beauty and helped by the perspective of remembering that life is short. It calms me, somehow, and makes the day-to-day challenges seem like not such a big deal. I was able to drive to the cemetery with a solid feeling of being cared about and that what I was going to do was a good thing, and of being part of a family, a part of history, independent and sometimes alone, but always connected.

When I arrived, I drove through the big stone gates and stopped at the bins full of authorized flower holders. I had brought some flowers from my garden and knew that my brother would be bringing some, too, along with tools for cutting the grass—a contrast of soft, pretty, fragrant blooms and practical, sharp knives. I was pleased that I could follow the winding roads and go right to where Grandma and Grandpa are; it's a big place and easy to get lost in.

When I pulled up alongside the area where their graves are, I saw that someone else was there, by a big stone, right next to Grandma and Grandpa's little stones. A woman was lying on her back on a bright red blanket with what sounded like a church service blaring from her car radio. I was a little annoyed. I'd been looking forward to a quiet arrival, alone, with just the sound of the birds and my memories, and here was a person just a few feet away that I couldn't avoid.

She sat up when she heard my car door close, and stood when I walked over. I saw that she was about my age and looked very sad. My attitude changed from annoyance to curiosity.

"Who are you here visiting?" I asked quietly.

"My dad. He died in April," just two months ago. "That's his funeral service," she continued, indicating the sound coming from the car.

"Oh, my father died years ago, but I know how you must feel," I replied.

And then her arms lifted slightly and I reached out and we hugged warmly, just two humans who both knew the grief of losing our fathers and how lonely that is and how it makes you grown-up in a new way you'd never imagined before, and we connected on that deep level without even knowing each other's names.

She asked me to take her picture by the family stone, next to the purple flowers she had placed there before I arrived. I told her I was visiting my grandparents and that I was meeting my brother, who seemed to be running late. She invited me to sit and listen with her to the service, and I thought maybe she wanted a little company, someone to share her experience with. So I sat down about ten feet away on the warm grass, and listened as her brother spoke about what a wonderful man her father had been, how he loved to dance with her mother, how he loved jazz music, how he had been an engineer who built many bridges and buildings in the area.

She told me little things about her family as the service went along. At one point she began to sniffle and I knew she was crying. I looked over and she looked at me, and she shook her head and said, "I don't know what I'm doing, telling my whole life to a stranger." And I said what I was truly feeling then: "Yes, but it doesn't really feel like strangers, does it?" She smiled and said no, and I smiled back.

The service ended with a very cheerful jazzy version of "When the Saints Go Marching In," and as the last bits of music played, I stood up, thinking that perhaps my brother was there and not being as lucky as I was in finding the right spot, driving around a bit wondering how to find me. I told her I was going to walk toward the entrance to see if Todd was searching for the right place, and we said goodbye as she packed her blanket and camera into her car. Sure enough, I walked over toward the main buildings and just as

I was peering around a tree, Todd drove up, rolled down his window, and said, "I was just realizing I didn't quite know where it was, and then I saw you." I pointed toward where my car was parked, and turned to walk back through the maze of monuments and trees to meet him there.

Todd and I sat down by the graves and began to work at clearing the overgrown grass from the granite stones, flush with the ground; they're not easily noticed, those small flat stones, and I had walked up and down the rows a bit to find them before he arrived. We put our flowers into the containers, one by each stone, and sat together, working for a few minutes. Todd told of going to two great Prince concerts that week, and then, inevitably, our talk turned to memories of our family . . . both good ones and not-so-good ones. We talked about how important but difficult it is to reconcile ourselves on a deeper level to things that happened when we were kids, how our parents did their best but still failed us in various ways, how we are coming to understand that their parents did the same with them.

Later, after we'd both gone home, I found myself thinking about my time at the cemetery, and how the two encounters I had were like two ends of the relationship spectrum: one simple, one complicated; one brand new and the other as old as my life; one mostly silent and the other full of talk; one brief and unexpected, one long and unavoidable; one a stranger, one a family member. But in both encounters, there was depth, genuine feeling and presence, and to each I brought myself as I was *that* day: sensitive and vulnerable, yet strong, with open heart and mind, feeling fully human and fully myself and fully centered in my own being.

How Do You Get to an Open Heart?

In the weeks before that day at the cemetery, I had some other kinds of days; hard ones full of pain and loneliness. On the outside I looked tired and messy; on the inside, I felt tired and messed up. I was exhausted from the roiling river of "breakup" emotions that had been moving through me.

Have you ever had days like that? Days when, instead of feeling hopeful, you feel sort of hopeless? Days when, instead of feeling open to the possibilities of life and love and friendship, the difficulties of a relationship make you feel as if your heart is closing in on itself? Most people do, at one time or another, and it can be just as hard when you're an adult as it is when you're a teen. On those hard days, I was lonely here in my house; I felt isolated from everyone, as if no one else could understand. My brain was filled with the nagging question of what to do: let it go? Call him and fight about it some more? Ask him to keep trying? Wait? Look for someone new?

By the time of the cemetery day, though, I had also come to feel some other things: strong, because I chose to end this relationship that wasn't working for me; grateful to a coworker who helped me realize that I needed to focus more on the friendship aspect of all my relationships; determined to get through this, to feel my feelings but choose wisely how to act on them; and renewed in my sense of my own worth as a person.

Three things helped me move through the storm: a book, a memory of an old friend's advice, and a reminder from my counselor.

Moving Through the Storm

The book that helped me so much is called *Coming Apart: Why Relationships End and How to Live Through the Ending of Yours* (2000). The writer, Daphne Rose Kingma, is a marriage and family therapist who tells of what she has learned in her years of helping clients through the ending of relationships. While she agrees that this is a very painful thing, she also brings hope to her readers. She points out that if we view all types of relationships as having cycles and reasons for being, and seasons for existing, and at times good reasons to end—we can learn from our relationships and then move on if and when the time is right.

What her book has taught me is that if I work on both my feeling and my thinking, I can move through the pain and hurt to a more balanced perspective on my part and the other person's part in both the good and the bad of the relationship. This applies equally to romances, friendships, and family ties. When you are hurting because a relationship is ending, maybe you'll find this approach valuable, too.

One of the most helpful parts of the book is a set of five writing exercises at the end, which she calls "rituals for parting." Although at first they seemed a little strange and artificial, I decided that I would commit myself to doing all of them, like doing emotional homework. So I spent time every day for a week working on them, writing in my journal my answers to these questions:

1. How did you fall in love (or become friends)?
2. What was the first clue you got that things might not work out?
3. What gifts did you give and receive in the relationship?
4. Looking back, what did you learn from this relationship?
5. What are you angry about and what are you grateful for?

I was surprised that sticking to the format, even though it felt forced at times, helped me process my thoughts *and* my feelings. Most important were the exercises about gifts and about what I learned. They helped me see that for me, for each of us, there are new, important things to learn about life and living well at every age and stage. And very often, that learning comes to us through our relationships with other people.

In the case of my breakup, despite the negative aspects of the relationship that brought it to a close, I could admit, after doing the exercises, that he had helped me become more independent, more proud of who I am. He showed me how to accept and embrace my playfulness and my creative side and helped me be more confident in myself. He liked my writing and my singing, and he encouraged me to work with him creatively on music, songwriting and recording.

I found that through reading the book, working on the exercises, and learning how to *think* differently about the relationship that my feelings changed, too. I still have moments of anger and hurt, but they are balanced by good memories, gratefulness, and acceptance.

Advice from an Old Friend

I haven't seen her in a long time, but when we worked together some years ago, my coworker, Liane, was my closest confidante. The greatest legacy of that friendship is a question she taught me to ask myself when I'm upset, confused, or in pain about my life, and can't seem to figure out what to do.

It is, "What would you say to a friend who was going through this?"

I asked myself that question one Saturday morning recently, when I woke up feeling low and lonely. And here is what I answered:

"I would hug her and reassure her that she is lovable, that she is good, that the low feelings are not her, that she can feel them and then let them subside. I would tell her to value her friends and family members who care about her, and to go ahead and do the things she thinks will bring her comfort, like take hot sudsy baths, or sit in the sunshine by a river, or go shopping at a bookstore. I'd tell her to spend some time alone, but to not forget to say yes to some invitations from friends to go do things that take her mind off herself and her feelings. I'd tell her to take a few moments each day to think about the blessings she has in her life right now."

Well, if I do say so myself, that sounded like good advice. It certainly helped me figure out what to do that day. I mentally let myself off the hook of doing chores; the laundry sat, grass kept growing, dirty dishes piled up. I walked to the bookstore and bought myself a new mystery novel. On the way home, I picked up some of my favorite foods at the grocery store. After unplugging the phone, I made myself a tray with a nice snack on it, and took it and my book to the bathtub. I filled the bath with hot water and added bubble bath and scented powders. Then I settled in to snack and read and relax. Later, when I got out (when the water finally got cold!), I felt calmer and more in touch with myself.

When I sit and think about it now, it strikes me as a very mysterious thing. Where did that wisdom come from? I asked myself the question, and suddenly I just knew the answers, heard them quietly in my mind. And I send a silent thank-you to Liane, for in the process of asking and answering, I found some of the keys to getting back to good, to centering, to regaining my sense of my self and my balance.

The next time you're struggling, try asking yourself the same question. What advice would you give a friend in your situation? Maybe you'd suggest that he let off some steam by snowboarding or write about problems in a journal. Maybe you'd recommend time alone listening to music, or maybe you think socializing with

friends would be a better idea. If you offer yourself the same con-
sideration you'd give a friend, you may be surprised by your own
good ideas.

Treasure Yourself First

Besides reading the book and remembering that good advice, I also
went to visit my counselor right around the time of the breakup.
I told her all the things that were going on with me, about the breakup and my other friend and family relationships and my work and
home life. And when I was done, when I told her I was looking for
her good advice, she said this:

"You know how when you go on an airplane, the flight attendants always go through the instructions for what to do in case of
a loss of cabin pressure? They tell you that if oxygen levels in the
cabin drop, oxygen masks will drop down in front of you from under
the overhead compartments. They demonstrate how to pull the
mask down to your face, secure it around the back of your head, and
then breathe from it. And then they say, 'If you are traveling with
a child or someone else who needs your help, secure your own mask
first, then help the other person.' What you need to do now, Kay,
is secure your own mask first."

Her point to me, then, was to focus away from others and my
relationships with others, and work on my relationship with myself.
And I took that thought away with me as I left her office and began
to think about what it might mean.

I realized that I had let the bad feelings about the end of one
relationship turn into bad feelings about myself. So I tried to turn
things around and be a friend to myself.

I reminded myself that just because one relationship ended,
that didn't mean I was a bad person; that being with a partner isn't
the sole measure of having a good life; that I had a number of other

close relationships in my life; that I deserved the same respect and kindness I give to my friends when they are in trouble; that I had many good qualities and interests and talents, just like everyone else, and I could spend my alone time taking care of myself and working on my writing and my singing and my own chores and tasks; and that by caring for myself, I would also be preparing for the time in the future when someone new could enter my life.

And it worked. I experienced those positive thoughts like pure oxygen; I could breathe again.

So on the day I went to the cemetery, I was able to get to a place of responding from my open, kind, true self, because these three things—the book, the question, and the reminder to care for myself— had helped me regain my balance.

Are there books, questions, and reminders that you have discovered along your own path that work this way for you? If not, feel free to borrow mine as you keep looking for your own inspiring words, insights, and ideas. The important thing is not how you get there, but that you recognize when you're feeling out of balance and take some action to get back in balance.

Don't Put Your Weight on a Moving Foot

I learned about the importance of balance more deeply and in a strong, useful way when I took a class in Tai Chi Chuan. It's a martial art because all the movements of it can be used in combat, but for most people it's mainly about self-defense, about turning an aggressor's strength back on her or him. And when you practice it, it is about balance and strength, about being stable and rooted at all times. It is very graceful, slow, and fluid, and it feels really good to do it and to do it simultaneously with the rest of the class.

Anyway, one of the things you wind up doing pretty often is

standing with your knees bent, with all your weight on one foot while you pick up and move the other foot to a new position. The mistake that most beginners make is that they shift their weight too soon, before they have planted their foot in the new place. If you do that in combat, you make yourself vulnerable to being pushed over or knocked off balance, because by putting your weight partly on that moving foot, you have made your stance unstable.

Try it. Stand up with your feet about shoulder-width apart. Relax your body and feel your weight evenly distributed over your two feet. Now shift your weight to just your left foot; feel your weight binding that foot to the ground, and imagine your foot putting down roots into the ground, like a strong tree. When you pick up your right foot, it will feel light and free, because there is no weight on it; choose a spot at what would be two o'clock on a clock, about a foot away from you, and move your foot there; you can place your right foot with great control and gracefulness anywhere because it is light and your weight is firmly on your left foot and leg, with knee bent. Keep your weight on the left until your right foot is firmly on the ground, then slowly bend your right knee and shift so your weight is once again evenly distributed between your two feet. You should be feeling strong and stable.

when i act on one of those impulses of escape or extreme measures, it's not making a choice about what to do; it's like crashing toward something, and i usually land with a thump.

Try it the other way now, with the beginner's mistake. Once you pick up your right foot and move it toward that spot a foot away, start to shift your weight toward that foot before you put it down. See what happens? Did you feel the difference? You begin to fall toward your right foot, and you land harder than you planned to. It is in that moment of falling that you are most vulnerable, because you have let go of your balance and stability. An opponent could easily shove you and knock you down because your weight is over your moving foot.

So what the teacher told us over and over was, "Don't put your weight on a moving foot." I came to realize that this is very good advice for living, too, not just for doing Tai Chi.

Here's how it works for me: When my emotions are strong and I'm feeling reactive, like doing something drastic or extreme, when my feelings and thoughts are going fast, whirling, and changing moment to moment, the situation is similar to that moment of falling. When I act on one of those impulses of escape or extreme measures, it's not really making a choice about what to do; it's like crashing toward something, and I usually land with a thump. I remind myself that my riled-up state is like that moving foot, and I shouldn't place my weight on any of those impulses until I feel solid and stable.

It also works when I'm dealing with other people. I try to use my perception to feel out whether they are stable or moving feet. When a friend or coworker seems to be reacting strongly or changing rapidly and unpredictably, going fast from one state to another (like the kind of person who is happy one minute and angry the next), I think of that person as a moving foot. And it might knock me off balance to put any psychic/emotional weight on them. That reminds me to keep my own boundaries up, to focus on centering myself, keeping myself strong and stable.

Looking toward the Future

As I set aside the pain of the past, think about my current relationships with friends and family, and look ahead to the possibility of a new love relationship in the future, that idea of balance is the one I want to carry with me. Yes, there has been pain and confusion, hurt and anger in my various relationships. But there have been many close and wonderful times, too: delightful times of dating, growing closer; good years of marriage; friendships that are long-lasting and deep, and friendships that arise just when I need them and then later drift apart; times when my siblings and I have pulled together to be there for each other and to provide a kind of under-standing that no one else can.

I see now that my relationships and my view of them some-times get out of balance. There have been times when I have only wanted to be with my friends and to ignore my family. There have been times when I only want to be with a boyfriend and ignore my other friends. Times when I want my friends to ignore their own needs and spend more time meeting mine! I have given too much in some relationships and put up with getting too little in return. In others, we have both given a lot at the beginning, only to have that fade over time. I still struggle a bit with balancing my needs for alone time and my needs for time with friends, my desire to be independent in a relationship but also to be intimate and close.

My friend Mark and I were e-mailing about this recently, and my friend Terri and I were talking about it, too. It felt so good to have these two friends, one married and one single (as well as my brothers and sister and a few other good friends), to talk it all over with, and I had an unexpected memory of the place back in the sev-enties where Terri and I met Mark, where it was easy to find good, caring people to talk things over with.

When Mark and Terri and I were teenagers, growing up in Sioux Falls, there was a place we could go where we could always just be ourselves—the youth room at Our Savior's Lutheran Church. This was my family's church, where we went to services every week and I sang in the youth choir. The youth pastor, Ray Engh, was a wonderful, warm man who wanted to make sure that we kids had somewhere to go that was both safe and fun, where we could be accepted for who we were. So he arranged for a room in the church basement to be fixed up with music and a pool table and comfy chairs, and set up times for it to be open on Wednesday and Friday nights and Sunday afternoons.

Quite a mixture of kids went there; you didn't have to belong to the church to go. Some were straight and some were gay, some were from rich neighborhoods and some from poorer ones; there were goody-goody types, druggies, nerdy straight-A students, and others who were like me, trying out belonging in all the different groups at different times. But we were all welcome, and we formed many unusual friendships over games of Crazy Eights, helping each other with homework, playing Ping-Pong, and so on. We'd use it as a base, where we could meet up with other kids without having to make a lot of plans; we'd meet there on Sundays to go to the Palisades Park on the river (packing ourselves into the few cars we had between us); we'd go there for early-morning breakfasts together

looking for balance: between intimacy and independence, caring for another person and caring for myself.

on Wednesdays. It was a place to go on a Friday night to goof around and play music and laugh or cry or complain about our parents and about school and about having boyfriends or girlfriends or not having them—it was great. I felt connected there; I felt I belonged.

As I think back, I realize the youth room was a place where the "peer pressure" (I didn't think of it as pressure at the time!) was pushing me in a good direction, toward fun, toward caring relationships, toward honesty. I was also spending some time searching for that feeling of connectedness and belonging in other groups and other places. One was an arcade downstairs from the shop downtown where I had my first paying job. I remember the first time I walked in and was introduced to some of the long-haired boys and punker girls. I was shy, as always, but they seemed to accept me without question and invited me to play foosball and pinball with them, and eventually to join them outside to smoke pot. When I refused, they were cool with that. But the more I hung out with them, the more curious I got about trying it; I didn't recognize that subtle curiosity about what the group was doing as "peer pressure," either. My need for a feeling of belonging made me blind to the "pressure" that pushed me in a negative direction, toward taking the seemingly small steps that later led to taking serious chances with drinking and partying.

In both places and groups, I was seeking a feeling of belonging and being connected. And I realized lately that I've been trying to recreate that same feeling in my adult life. It's my home now that is my base, and I have to reach out to form connections with people rather than having them just exist in a place I visit. I find my place and my intimacy with people in different groups—coworkers, high school friends, college friends, new friends, siblings—but I'm very conscious now of choosing to be with the people who help me to be and do my best. Not because I'm trying to be "good" or because I'm being a snob or something, but because it makes life a lot better and easier when I can get a little help (you could call it positive pressure) from my friends and family members. All those different relationships form a strong web of support and love that I'm connected to, and the connections are strong, whether I have a romantic relationship in my life or not.

When I do have another romantic relationship, I'm going to be looking for that feeling of belonging and being connected, but I'm also going to be thinking a lot about mutual help in life and about balance: between having a life together and having a life apart, between sharing current interests and exploring new ones; between caring for the other person and being true to myself, my dreams, and my goals.

Learning Is Vital to Relationships

I've learned a lot through relationships and about relationships over my 46 years so far—relationships with friends, with family, and with partners—including that:

- They are sometimes complicated and sometimes simple.
- Each one has a reason and a season.
- Sometimes relationships have breaks in them, and while some breaks can be repaired, some cannot or should not.
- It's important to pay attention to both my thoughts and my feelings about my connections with other people.

All these things I've learned mainly through experience, through having relationships and living through the good times and the bad times and the confusing in-between times. But I've also realized that there are skills to be used in relationships, and I sure didn't learn all of the skills I needed by the time I was 18, or 25, or 37, or even 46.

I remember very clearly one occasion during my later teens when my mom gave me some valuable teaching about communication and getting acquainted. She and my dad and I were spending some time up at our lake cabin in northern Minnesota. One evening Mom and I drove together into Duluth, the nearest city of any size, to attend a chamber music concert. I wasn't completely thrilled about chamber music per se, but the concert was being held in a huge mansion on the shore of Lake Superior, and I wanted to see that, plus there was going to be a wine-and-cheese reception afterward. (It was legal for 18-year-olds to drink alcohol at that time.) The music and the setting in the mansion were lovely, but once I got my glass of wine and nibble of cheese, I felt nervous and bored around all these people I didn't know. I wandered out onto the terrace overlooking the lake to imagine for a few moments myself living in that mansion. Then I went back in. I saw Mom was talking with someone, and I lurked on the sidelines wishing we could just go.

When Mom finished talking to that fellow, I went up to her and asked if we could leave. But she was having fun and wanted to mingle a little more. When I said I didn't know any of these people and didn't know how to mingle, she said, "Oh, well, it's not so hard. Let's just stay long enough to talk with one more person, and I'll show you how." I grudgingly agreed, and so Mom and I approached a pleasant-looking middle-aged woman, with rather pouffy blonde hair and a formal black dress, and I stood watching and listening as Mom said hello and struck up a conversation.

The other woman responded in a friendly way, though with rather a strong German accent. Mom asked the woman where she was from and what she did for work. We learned that she had come from Germany after World War II and was now a music teacher at a college in Duluth. Using that information to find things they might have in common, Mom told her that my dad was a professor at Augustana College in Sioux Falls, South Dakota. Well, this woman's face lit up and she exclaimed, "Oh, I went to Augustana! Who is your husband?!" And when Mom told her Dad's name, she said, "Oh, I had such a crush on him when I was in school! All that lovely red hair!" Mom and I just looked at each other for a second and then burst out laughing, and the three of us had such fun talking— and the two of us had such fun teasing Dad when we got back to the cabin. And to think I would never have had that delightful surprise and shared fun with Mom if she hadn't offered to teach me the basics of how to mingle with strangers.

Since that simple lesson about starting relationships and that striking illustration of the potential benefits of developing relationship skills, I've made a point of doing more intentional learning. I'm sure there will be more as time goes by, but here are some important ones that I really value now.

Learning how to resolve conflicts. I remember being utterly amazed at age 19 when I had a fight with a friend and she called the next day to ask if we could talk about it. I didn't know you could do that! In my family growing up no one talked over their disagreements. They would just hold it in and hold it in, until eventually they would burst out with their anger, and there would be a loud fight, followed by one person finally stomping away. Then it was never discussed again. Lots of stress, tension, and pain can build up when people deal with each other that way.

It's not easy, because it's very uncomfortable and unnatural to me, but I've learned something about how to talk things over. I've learned, mainly with help from some of my friends, like Jenni and Mary Ellen, and my sister, Nancy, that we can acknowledge when we've hurt each other's feelings, that we can each take responsibility for our own part in the hurt and misunderstanding, and that if we each approach it in a spirit of wanting the relationship to be repaired, we can do that.

Learning how to talk. I've learned that there are many ways to say something, ways that are easily understood, ways that are hurtful, ways that are confusing. I've read books by people like Deborah Tannen, who has done fascinating research on the different ways that women and men tend to think and talk. The research looks for the bigger patterns in communication among people, and of course individuals each have their unique ways, but knowing the big patterns can often lead to individual insights. She points out that all humans, both women and men, need intimacy and independence, but that in heterosexual relationships, women tend to focus on intimacy and men on independence. This difference can lead to common misunderstandings.

For example, friends or couples sometimes clash when one (often the man) makes plans without checking in with the other (often the woman). From the man's point of view, he might be thinking that checking in about plans is like having to ask permission, which would mean to him a loss of independence. From the woman's point of view, she might be thinking that checking in is acknowledging that their lives are intertwined and so the actions of one have an impact on the other; to her, the lack of checking in might mean a loss of intimacy in the relationship.

Learning about this larger pattern and how easy it is for people to misunderstand each other, even when they are in a loving relationship, has made me a lot more careful about what I say and especially *how* I say it.

I've also learned about how to be tactful and diplomatic (most of the time ☺), rather than just blurting out my first reaction. And I've learned that I sometimes need to take a time-out, to allow my strong feelings to subside, before coming back together with someone to talk things through.

Learning about respect. I've also found, through many experiences, that important relationships come to me at times when I least expect them. I believe that there are times when people come into our lives for reasons that are mysterious, even cosmic, that some meetings are simply meant to be, and that we can't know when that is going to happen. So I choose to believe what a character in one of my all-time favorite novels says: "The people we meet must be treated with infinite respect, for few of them arrive casually in our lives." (The book is The Clairvoyant Countess, by Dorothy Gilman.)

Certainly, some people seem to just pass through without making a ripple in my life's current. But I've had many experiences of what at first seemed chance meetings turning out to have great significance, so I keep it in mind that anyone I meet might become important to me—though it's easier said than done. At my best, I try to adopt an attitude toward each person that helps me be open to that possibility: My goal is to greet them with friendliness, listen to them with empathy, treat them with intentional kindness, be present with them when we are together, and respect their efforts to be and do their best, just as I wish for their respect for my efforts to be and do my best. (It is the attitude toward our fellow humans that many religious traditions say we should take, too—to love our neighbors as ourselves, to greet the divine element that is present in each person.)

I've received many benefits from choosing to take this attitude: I have had help from unexpected places when I've needed it; I've been able to work well with people I disagree with; and I've had small, lovely moments of joy.

Here is just one example of why I recommend it: When the office I work at was located in downtown Minneapolis, I had to pay to park my car every day in a big lot down the block. Most days that was easy and there was plenty of room. But on days when there was an afternoon game of the Minnesota Twins or the Minnesota Vikings at the nearby Metrodome, the parking lot got crowded and instead of just driving in and parking, we office workers had to sign in with one of the men who were roaming through the lot in bright orange vests, holding clipboards and figuring how to cram a few more cars in at $20 apiece.

One was an older man, old enough, anyway, to be my father, a retired fellow who did this work part-time. Unlike a lot of the other parking lot attendants, he was always friendly, and he seemed to like it when I was friendly back. We got into a habit of greeting each other; he would say, "Hello, Beautiful, how are you today?!" and I would say, "Hello, hello, how's the parking lot mess today!?" After some months of this, we started feeling like friends and gave each other a quick hug and a kiss on the cheek on those mornings when we met. We didn't know each other well, and we didn't talk much about our lives or families, but we welcomed those occasional moments of friendly greeting. He told me his nickname, Doob, and I called him that. I told him my name, but he said he'd rather just call me "Beautiful." That was fine with me!

When our company moved several years later, I was sad that I wouldn't see my parking-lot friend anymore. But every once in a while, I would drive by on my way to the new office location, and I would see him standing at the edge of the driveway into the parking lot. One day, I was feeling kind of low as I drove to work, and I saw him there. On an impulse I honked my horn, pulled over, and waved at him. At first, he didn't recognize me. But as he got closer, he did, and his face lit up, and he said, "Beautiful! Where've you been? How are you?!" He leaned in the window, and we hugged, and I told him okay, but work was getting me down, and he said, "Well, that's how life goes. Just you remember that I love you, and things will get better." Oh, that was nice. Just what I needed that morning.

I look for him every day now on my way to work. And occasionally, I still see him and honk the horn, and he comes over for a hello and a hug. Twenty seconds later I drive away, feeling good, and I guess he does, too.

It's a little thing, a small relationship, but a good one. It forms a strand in the web of relationships that I have in my life at any one time.

Learning when to spend more time with myself. When I'm unhappy about my relationships with others, when I don't seem to have enough of them, or when one or more of them seems filled with misunderstanding or boredom or anger, I sometimes find myself consumed with questions about the other person: Why doesn't he understand me? Why doesn't she treat me the way I treat her? Why doesn't he trust me? Why does she say those things that hurt my feelings?

I've learned a technique that helps me work through those times. I try to turn those questions around so that I'm asking about myself rather than the other person—because, after all, I can't control or change other people, but I can always work on myself. So I turn them around and ask: How well do I understand myself? How well do I explain myself and my thoughts and feelings to others? Why do I say and do the things I say and do? Why am I feeling hurt? What is making me feel as though I don't belong?

And in the process of questioning, I often find that there is something out of whack in my relationship with myself. And it never fails that when I work on that—when I spend time figuring out my own sensitivities and triggers, my own desires and needs, my own actions and beliefs—it forms the solid ground from which I can stand strong and reach out to others. Because when I'm right with myself, it's much, much easier to put things right and keep things right with everyone else.

I came across a coffee mug the other day that helps me keep this whole thing in mind. It's a deep midnight-blue color with these words printed in white: I AM, THEREFORE I BELONG. The mug was from a membership drive at Minnesota Public Radio some years ago and was intended to encourage people to financially support the station. But I use it many days as a reminder that I don't have to do anything special to belong to the human race, all I have to do is be who I am, the best "me" that I can. The calm, centered feeling I get as a result is what allows me to reach out to others with an open heart and mind.

· 5 ·
If You're Still Breathing, You're Not Finished

Does life ever just freak you out to the point that you can't figure out what to do or how to handle it? Have you ever felt inside that there was nothing you could do to fix a situation that happened to you or that you'd gotten yourself into? That you might as well give in and give up, because things were so bad that there was no hope left?

By the time I was 16, I had had that experience. I want to tell the story, but I also feel as though I should add a little caution, like the ones on those car commercials that show stunt drivers doing amazing tricks with the cars while the little print at the bottom says, "Don't try this at home." Here's what happened:

I was hanging out with several different groups of friends. The thing they all had in common was that we wanted to do everything we weren't supposed to do. We smoked cigarettes, we drank alcohol, we tried pot and other drugs, we stayed out later than our parents allowed, and many of us also started having sex.

Part of all that came from wanting new experiences and just being sort of rebellious; part of it was the society at the time, which encouraged, "if it feels good, do it" and "free love"; but part of it, too, came from discovering that what we'd been told about these "bad" things wasn't the whole story. We were told, for example, that sex was something we weren't supposed to do, end of story. But no one had been honest with us about what it was like. Nobody said that it felt good to hug and kiss and touch and be touched. So when I started getting into dating and having experiences of doing more than kissing and hugging, it made me suspect that the rules about not doing it were just made by adults trying to stop people from having a good time.

I wanted to keep having those feelings. Besides, the boy I was dating wanted to and pressured me to . . . so, as I've already mentioned, I started to have sex (and unprotected sex, too; contraception wasn't talked about as much in the seventies, and it wasn't as easily available as it is now, either). I felt mixed up and guilty about my sexual experiences, confused by the contradiction of strong desires and societal messages about how important it is to be sexy, and rules from school and church about it being a bad thing. I didn't think it through very clearly at the time, though; then I just wanted to be loved, and despite my unhappy first experience, I thought that if a boy wanted to have sex with me it meant he loved me.

Well, maybe you can imagine how wrong I was about that, and maybe you can guess what happened. I woke up one morning and when I got out of bed, I felt sick, as if I was going to throw up. The next day, it happened again. I realized I hadn't had my period for six weeks, about two weeks late, and the thought hit me that I might actually be pregnant. I was scared and embarrassed and didn't want to believe it was true. Finally, I told my friend Terri what I was worried about, and she helped me find a clinic where I could get a pregnancy test after school. It was positive.

I was so upset; crying, worrying, afraid, confused about what to do, feeling sure I was too young to have a baby and be a parent and, most of all, terrified about telling my mom. I knew I'd have to, though; there was no way I could figure this one out on my own. But Mom and I didn't always get along that well, and I was pretty sure she'd be furious. I left the clinic in a daze and went to see my boyfriend to tell him what had happened. It was a very hard discussion to have. He was shocked and upset and nervous, but he didn't back away from me. He asked me if I wanted to get married. That was very decent of him to ask; he was taking his share of the responsibility for the situation. But I immediately answered no; it didn't seem like a good solution to me. He was in college and I was still in high school and neither of us could support ourselves, let alone a family. I didn't know what I *did* want to do, but getting married wasn't it.

I went home late that afternoon and somehow managed to have supper with my family. All through the meal, I sat there trying to look normal, but feeling nervous and upset inside and wondering how in the world I was going to tell Mom. After supper, I hung around the kitchen while she was doing the dishes, working up the nerve to tell her. As she washed the pots and pans at the end, and I still hadn't said anything, she started talking. She said how she'd been thinking about my future, that soon I'd be able to go off on my own and go to college and how she thought I'd enjoy that much more than high school and learn so much and meet new people, and that she was excited for me about how my life was going to be.

Oh, God, I just lost it inside. Here she was talking about my future, and I was convinced that I didn't have one at all. To me, my life was stopped dead right there, in that yellow-walled kitchen, her at the sink and me sitting at the table. It truly seemed as though there was no way out. And finally I started to cry. She heard me, turned around, and asked me what was wrong—and I finally managed to choke out the words.

"Mom, I'm pregnant."

My mother surprised me then. She really came through for me at a time when I needed her desperately. She didn't get angry or yell, she just looked at me, took off her rubber gloves, walked over from the sink, said, "Oh, honey," and put her arms around me in a tight hug. "Come on, we'll go talk on the porch."

For a while, she just sat with me, holding me while I cried out my pain and anguish. She asked me who the boy involved was, but

my life was stopped dead right there, in that yellow-walled kitchen, mom at the sink and me at the table.

I wouldn't tell her. I thought she'd make a scene with him, and he and I had already talked about it. I told her he had said we could get married if I wanted to, but that I thought I was way too young for that kind of commitment.

She asked me what I wanted to do. The words and fear all tumbled out together: "I don't know . . . I'm too young . . . it feels like life would be over if I had a baby." It was a huge relief just to speak those fears aloud and to have her be strong and caring, to have her be there for me.

She didn't take over and tell me *what* to do, but she took charge for me and taught me *how* to figure it out. She told me to go ahead up to my room early and try to get some sleep. She said that the next day we would look at the options and talk them over; and she gave me a book to read that included stories of other girls and women who had had unexpected pregnancies, that simply and clearly talked about the need for and process of making a careful, wise decision, that described the various options and discussed the many ethical, religious, and legal aspects of those options.

Suddenly, my life was not over. I had someone older and wiser to help me. I had access to information and help with how to make a decision. And I had the new knowledge that there were options, there were people who'd gone through this before me, and there were solutions. Or at least ways to move forward. With my mom's help, I was able to see the options, weigh the consequences, and make my own decision about my life and my future.

What did I learn in the process? I learned that I had been taking an awful lot of risks with my health and my future without understanding what the consequences could be. I learned that people can surprise you, can come through for you when you least expect it. I learned that being allowed to take responsibility for acting on my own beliefs—being treated like a grown-up who can make grown-up decisions based on her own personal values—was something I liked, even though it was the hardest decision I've ever had to make. And I learned that even though sometimes life freaks me out, I can deal with it.

There's Always Something I Can Do

At that time, a new view of life opened up for me. When I think back, I picture it in my mind this way: Up until then, I had always lived as if life was a railroad track and I was a train. But it was like one of those funny scenes in cartoons, like the one in the British claymation movie *The Wrong Trousers*, when a character lays down track right in front of the train as it's going. I didn't see very far, just barreled ahead and hoped there would be new track each day for my train to run on, laid there by some mysterious character other than myself.

Then I started to have glimpses of what looked like tracks stretching way out in front of me. Eventually, I realized that I was really only a short way out of the station. I could see from my engine window a vast rolling prairie, with mountains in the distance, and tracks leading out into the future. And not just one set going in one direction; there were junctions coming up, places where two tracks diverged from one another, and though I couldn't always see what was around the bends or on the other side of the tunnels, I was the one who would decide which of the tracks to take. And I realized that there were going to be many, many times in my life when I would have to make hard decisions about which way to go; this wasn't the only one, it was just the first.

I learned that there are always options, choices. Choosing one set of tracks over the other doesn't mean that the tracks stop or that there won't be more junctions up ahead. I discovered that I could change, that I could ask for help with the big decisions, I could think things through and take action. And I've discovered since then that there is a deep satisfaction in knowing there are always choices and that the decisions are mine. I can keep learning, and learning more deeply, for my whole life.

If Things Get Really Bad

Have you ever seen the show *Cell Dogs* on Animal Planet? My friend, Terri, had been telling me how great this show was, and she was right. (By the way, this is the same Terri from stories about my youth. We met when we were 13 and we've been friends now for more than 30 years!) In case you haven't seen the show, here's the deal: It takes place in prisons all across the country where they have started a program with convicted prisoners training dogs. The dogs are rescued from shelters, where they've been placed because they have behavior problems. Expert animal trainers teach the prisoners how to train the dogs, and each participating prisoner lives 24 hours a day, 7 days a week with a dog, feeding it, caring for it, working with it. When the training is done, the successful dogs go out into the world to be helper dogs for people who are deaf; they can turn on light switches, alert their owners to a ringing telephone or a knock on the door, that sort of thing.

I thought that was such an amazing idea, to pull all those pieces together to create good in the world: to save the dogs, to provide the prisoners with new skills and the love of their dogs, to end up with well-trained dogs to help more people. And the image that really sticks with me is this: One of the prisoners on the episode I saw was a big, tough guy with tons of tattoos and huge muscles. He talked in the interviews about how he'd been in gangs and done a lot of criminal things in his life, but how learning to take care of the dog and having that dog love him and depend on him had changed him. He was more in touch with his feelings, he had a goal and a purpose in his life, even in prison. Every week he would take his dog to visit the prisoners who were in solitary confinement. These prisoners were some of the hardest and toughest—rapists, molesters, murderers. The kind of people you might think had done things so bad that their lives were just over.

But they showed this prisoner take his dog to one of the cell doors. The inmate inside had being convicted of a violent murder. He was held in a small cell and rarely allowed out with the other inmates. He could only reach a little bit to the world outside his cell through a slot in the door covered with a metal flap. You could see him peering out, looking tough and angry. But when that other prisoner came around with his dog, that murderer's face changed. His tough sneer melted away, and he looked softer and kinder, al-most like the little boy he once was, as he reached through the slot to pet the friendly dog. He smiled—and it seemed as if he had been able to set aside the hurt and betrayal and anger of his former life and respond with love and warmth to a lick on the hand from a dog.

For the inmates who are learning to care for and train the dogs, the program lets them see that even though they are in prison, life isn't over; there are options and choices and chances to learn. Their train may be limited to the prison tracks, but there are possibilities, ways to keep going and growing.

Throughout your life, you come up against situations that are difficult: from a misunderstanding with a friend to a fight with a boyfriend or girlfriend; or you make situations difficult by breaking a promise or lying or blaming others for your own problems or refusing other people's help. You have feelings and desires and impulses, and you choose to act on some of them, and sometimes you get careless or you screw up: You choose to steal, to have sex when you're not emotionally ready, to drink too much, to start smoking and then find it almost impossible to stop. In the most extreme situations, some people physically or emotionally hurt others.

What that image of the prisoner bringing his dog to his fellow prisoner in the cell reminds me, though, is that not one of us is done with our life until our life is done with us. We can make amends. We can say we're sorry, even if others aren't ready to forgive. We can try again and again. We can learn from the consequences and move on. We can trust that the tracks are stretching out ahead of us, even if we can't see where they are leading. We can accept the help of other people who can show us options and choices we may not have been able to see yet. And there is hope. There is always, always hope of joy to come. Because I am still breathing, and I am not finished yet.

· 6 ·
Every Day
Holds a Blessing
to Find

I often wake early these days, and one day recently I woke up early enough that I saw the sunrise over the nearby houses. It was a blaze of fire against a ceiling of dark gray clouds, and I remembered a time when I saw a sunrise when I was a kid.

I was in 3rd grade at Mark Twain Elementary in Sioux Falls. It was a big brick building with a nice playground and was only about six blocks away from my house, so I walked each day with the girls who lived next door and across the street.

We had a special class in music once or twice a week, as I recall. One day, the teacher told us that we would be listening in the next class to a piece of classical music that someone wrote about the sunrise. She said that if we could, we should watch a sunrise soon so that we'd be ready to listen to that music.

When I got home from school that day, I told my parents that my homework was to watch a sunrise. (I was a serious girl when it came to school. ☺)

My dad was an early riser, and he said we could go tomorrow. The following morning, he came into my room and woke me quietly, so my sister wouldn't wake up, in the darkness of early morning. I got up and dressed and came downstairs to the kitchen. He made hot chocolate for us, poured it in a thermos, put two mugs in a bag along with a couple of donuts, and then we went outside.

The air was cool but soft. It felt mysterious and secret in a rather exciting way to have this mission before us. Everyone else was asleep, but we were out doing something special. I felt like a small, nocturnal animal creeping through the dark. We were very quiet, like the world around us, and our car was the only one on the roads.

Our town was about 60,000 people at that time, and it didn't take long to drive south through the neighborhoods, past the businesses, to the edge of town and then out into the country, where we moved past fields and pastures and farms. Soon Dad turned east on a gravel road, and we could see the whole sky all around us, with no buildings in the way. The horizon was so low and dark, with just little trees and farmhouses here and there; above it, the whole bowl of the sky was beginning to lighten in color.

Dad pulled over and we parked facing east. It was chilly that morning, so we stayed in the car. What I remember is sitting there just watching the sky transform, sipping hot chocolate and eating our donuts, talking softly occasionally but mostly being quiet, absorbing the colors, seeing the change from subtle brightening to the emergence of blue, the hints of yellow and pink and red; the long, long time of the sun's coming and the suddenness of its leap up over the horizon; how the changing light changed everything we could see, how it brought color to the world, and shadows, and shape.

Our hot chocolate and donuts were gone, the sun was up, and Dad said, "Okay, shall we go home now?" And we did. We drove back the way we had come, but everything looked so different from that mysterious nighttime drive out; things were ordinary now, people were up and about, and the streets were busy with cars. We got home and all the other kids and Mom were up, and there was the usual bustling about and noise and breakfast and getting ready for school.

And the next day in music class, when the teacher asked who had been able to watch a sunrise, I proudly raised my hand, wanting to be the first one. I looked around to see who else had done it. Not only was I first, I was the *only* kid in class to raise her hand.

I realized at that moment, in a child's sort of way, that I had been lucky that Dad had made that happen for me.

It's Up to Me

The other morning, when I remembered about the sunrise, I reached back into my memory and found other inklings of this kind of joy: taking walks in the north woods and along a river with Mom and my brothers and sister; looking for agates at the beach; going as a family to Fourth of July band concerts and fireworks displays; hiking as an adult to the bottom of a beautiful red-rock canyon in New Mexico; working in my own garden to plant flowers the butterflies will like; and I realized that all of these are blessings that have formed a thread that has been running through my life for years and years.

I've found it's a strong and colorful thread. I can use it to bind the other things together; I can use it to follow through the twists and turns of my daily ups and downs, like the one the prince in the fairy tale follows to seek the princess in the middle of the maze.

Now, when I think of the sunrise with my dad, I realize what a lesson there is in that experience, though I didn't catch it deeply at the time. It's that on any day, at any time, we can choose to create and live a wonderful, deep experience, if we only take the time to notice our blessings, to experience them fully, to be open to them, and to appreciate them.

Another Lesson from Dad

As with every other one of the truths I know so far, there was the first time I came to know it, and then the time I had to spend trying to put it to use. In every case, more experiences brought me deeper understanding and forced the lesson to become more conscious.

In this case, by the time I got to my teens and then into my twenties, I had sort of forgotten about noticing and appreciating blessings. In the process of growing up, I'd found that life was sometimes much harder than I had expected. I had experienced disappointments in school, failures in work. I was never satisfied with what I had; I felt that life was cheating me, that I didn't get nearly enough good stuff, certainly not as much as other people did. I always wanted more, better, bigger, different.

And so life, and Dad, brought me another lesson in blessings. This one came when I was 28. I had made it through college and decided to be an editor and writer. After several years in Colorado,

i was trying to be independent, but finding it tough to handle.

another year in upstate New York, and some time in Massachusetts, I detoured back through South Dakota for a few weeks with Mom and Dad and eventually ended up in Minnesota, having taken a job for not very much money working for my uncle in the small town of Northfield. Yet another change in location and job and apartment in my continuing search for a life that felt good and right to me. I had left behind all my friends and immediate family, and I was lonely. The work I was doing was interesting but difficult, and brought barely enough income to pay my bills (including the rent for my not-so-nice apartment) and have a little left over for fun. I was trying to be independent, but finding it tough to handle. It just felt like a lot to be in charge of—too much sometimes. I was experiencing lots of new things at once, and that's hard, because new things at first often bring confusion and frustration with them and force you to learn new skills. In the process, usually, you make some mistakes.

One of the things that was new to me was having a car; I had just bought my first one, back in South Dakota before I moved to Minnesota. I'd never had a car before and didn't know a thing about taking care of it or fixing it if something went wrong. I worried about it all the time. And when something did go wrong—for example, I locked my keys in once—my reaction was along the lines of, "Eek, now what do I do?!" Another time I left the lights on all day in the middle of winter. When I came out of work, the battery was completely dead.

Dealing with my car always seemed like an ordeal.

I knew that August was the time for me to get new license plate stickers to show that I had paid the year's taxes on the car. I had been busy, though, and was late remembering about that. Since I had bought it in South Dakota and hadn't transferred it (or whatever you're supposed to do) to Minnesota, I called and asked my dad back home to take care of that and send them to me. I sent him a check and waited for the stickers, worrying that they would not be on time, and that I might get ticketed by the police for having expired tabs, ruining my perfect driving record and raising my insurance. Arrggh!

But Dad was always reliable. The next week after a hectic day at work, I came home knowing that I had lots of chores to do around the apartment. When I arrived, I found an envelope from my dad in the mail. Inside were the bright yellow stickers I needed to put on my license plates and a note from him on an index card:

INSTRUCTIONS

1. Go to kitchen and get two paper towels. Run a little water on one of the towels and keep the other one dry.

2. Take the two paper towels and the new stickers out to the car. Use damp paper towel to wipe off any dirt on old stickers.

3. Use damp paper towel to wipe off any moisture left on old stickers. Use dry paper towel to wipe off any moisture left on old stickers.

4. Listen to birds sing for ten minutes.

5. Peel new stickers off their backing and attach to proper place. Rub each thoroughly, especially around the edges, to be sure they stick well.

Oh, that just made me smile. I had been in such a hurried, stressed mode, and that funny set of instructions from Dad just changed everything. I smiled and laughed, and felt myself slow down inside and settle down, too. I decided I would follow the instructions exactly. So I put the new stickers in my back pocket, got the paper towels, one wet and one dry, and carried them down my creaky, narrow back stairs to the car out on the gravel driveway. I hadn't really noticed before, but it was a nice sunny day, not too humid, not very buggy.

I scrubbed each old sticker with the wet towel and dried with the dry one, and then scooted up onto the hood of the car, prepared to listen to the birds for the required ten minutes. I checked my watch, set the towels down beside me, folded my hands in my lap, and just sat there. I didn't hear any birds at first, but I noticed the feeling of the sun and the lightest possible breeze on my arms. My gaze moved to the garage next door and I noticed some of the paint was peeling off. I noticed the overgrown bushes beside the driveway, and thought how someday I'd like to have my own yard, and I would keep the bushes nicely trimmed so they'd look pretty. I started to notice tiny swaying movements in one of the bushes, and then heard a bird twitter in there. I heard other birds, a crow cawing down the street a ways, other birds seeming to answer the first one in a kind of mass twitter. As I listened, I looked up and watched as huge, billowing clouds scudded out from behind the cottonwood in the side yard. I noticed how brilliantly white they were, and how, if I kept watching one cloud, I could see it changing shape continuously.

The sun started to feel hot on my arm, and being a very fair-skinned Scandinavian, I have to be careful about not getting sunburned. So I looked at my watch to see if ten minutes had gone by.

Twenty minutes had passed. I hadn't even been aware of time, or my problems at work, or the pressure of all my chores and all the decisions about my life I was worried about.

I smiled again and jumped off the car. I reached into my back pocket, pulled out the stickers, and carefully put each one on, running my finger over the edges to be sure they would stay on.

I always smile when I think of that day. I'm smiling now as I write about it, having let my memories surface so I could live it over again in my imagination. Nowadays, I make sure I order the new tabs as soon as the notice comes in the mail. And every year, when I get the new stickers, I make it a ritual to do it the same way, and I remember my dad as I sit quietly listening to the birds, counting my blessings.

Life Is Short

I can only remember Dad now, because he died in 1995.

For weeks after his death, I was very sad, intensely caught up in the experience. But one of the things that became so utterly clear in those first few days, after the initial grief and the details of the funeral and all the family in town and the arrangements and everything, was a deep, deep knowledge of a new truth: Life is short.

Obviously, I didn't coin that phrase. But for each of us, there comes a time, often with the death of a parent or other close relative or friend, when we realize that death can come at any time, that it stops everything, and (most shocking of all) that it is going to happen to us someday, too.

Knowledge of life and death come slowly and gradually, over time. We begin to learn about them as little children, as our parents and siblings and friends tell us things, as we learn stories and songs that others have written about life and death, and as we experience our own life and the lives and deaths around us. I had known of death, I had even experienced deaths of others close to me (my favorite cat, a grandfather and a grandmother, a sweet uncle), but not until my father died did I get that sudden rush of how precious life is, how short, how impossible to grasp and hold onto; how inevitable death is and how quickly and suddenly it cuts you off, cuts off your life.

In the months and years after Dad died, each of us siblings was struck by that deep knowledge of how short life can be and used it to re-evaluate our lives. We made decisions about finding more satisfying, rewarding jobs, moving to different cities, going back to college, making new efforts in our relationships, following our dreams.

I also made a smaller decision: that I would try to notice and savor all the good things that came my way, because at any time my life could be over, and I wanted to be sure I got the most out of it that I could.

Now, for me, living a good life involves a lot of things, including doing work that feels important and worthwhile, learning new skills, appreciating and loving good friends, and many more. But one of the best steps I've ever taken toward a good life is learning to notice each blessing.

There's Always a Blessing to Find

In every single day, in every activity, in every moment, in every situation, there is a blessing to be found.

It may not be obvious; it may take quite a bit of looking, but it's there. Or maybe there are a lot, maybe more than you think. And looking for them is a good habit to get into. (I've gotten into lots of bad habits unintentionally, but this is one of the good habits I've chosen for myself and I've *worked* at making it a habit.) At first I had to write myself notes about it. I'd write on a sticky note and attach it to the bathroom mirror; or I'd make a poster and put it inside the fridge (I know this may sound weird, but it works for me ☺), so I'd find it when I got home from work and was starving and probably crabby. I don't have to think very hard about it now; after years of practice, I do it more naturally, easily, automatically.

There are mornings, though, when I wake up dreading the day ahead. Maybe I'm sad because I'm waking up alone instead of with someone to share breakfast with or a friendly cat to snuggle with. Maybe I know that I have to deal with a hard problem at work or that I have to lead a lot of meetings when I'd rather just work quietly. Maybe it's a day when I'm feeling overwhelmed by all the things I have to do, and they all feel piled up like a big mound on top of me.

I have come up with some rituals and routines that work for

me, that help me each day to renew my decision to notice each blessing. I like really good coffee, so I buy good coffee beans, and I get up each morning and stumble my way out to the kitchen to start heating the coffee water. Then I go into the living room and lay down on the carpet and stretch. I might do some sit-ups, I might use my little weights to work on my arms, I might turn on a yoga video or another exercise video, anything to get my blood and body moving and to get my breathing going. I do that until the kettle whistles. Then I grind the beans, make my coffee, add cream and sugar, and sit at the kitchen table by the window to savor it. I look out to see what kind of day it is. Then I reach for a book of daily meditations.

The one I like best is *The Unauthorized Starfleet Daily Meditation Manual: Going Boldly on Your Inner Voyage,* by Mark Stanley Haskett. Each day there is a quotation from characters on one of the *Star Trek* television shows (like Spock saying, "You must have faith that the Universe will unfold as it should," or Commander Riker saying, "The game isn't big enough unless it scares you a little"), which is followed by a few paragraphs of thoughts about what that quotation means and how it might give the reader an idea for living that day. The meditations all relate our inner selves and spirits to the larger world. They help me see that while I'm powerful in my own way in my own life, there's also always a great big universe out there, and that gives me a nice perspective to start the day with.

for me, each morning, it's a choice i can make.

After my morning shower and getting dressed for work, I always pause when I first step outside and focus on all my senses, one at a time. How does the air feel on my skin? How is the light falling on the garage door? What birds or squirrels, car engines or neighbors can I hear? What is the scent that is being carried to me on the breeze?

For me, each morning, it's a choice I can make. I can and do take an intentional, positive stance toward life, knowing that it gets difficult at times, that grief and confusion come to everyone, but that I can choose not to lose sight of what is wonderful, beautiful, and true, big or small. In grief, in sadness, in trouble, in exciting times, I can notice each rose, each beam of sunlight, each good feeling and true friend, each small success, each moment of glory or contentment, victory or strength, and choose to revel in that goodness for as long as it lasts.

It doesn't matter how you do it—coffee, a meditation, and some stretches is just the way I've found for myself. Maybe for you it's with a glass of juice and a favorite wake-up song while you look out the window; maybe it's with a shower and some small talk with someone in your family about your goals for the day. As long as you know you can make the choice, that you have the power to start yourself off well and intentionally look for the beauty and blessings in a day, you can put it into practice in whatever way works for you.

Suddenly as I write this I have a memory of one of the picture books I had when I was little. I don't know the name of it, but I can still see clearly in my mind some of the pictures. As I recall, the book tells the story of a grade school teacher in a poor neighborhood in a big city. One day, she is doing a lesson with the children about art, and they talk about what is beautiful, and she gives the children the homework assignment of coming back to class the next day to report on something beautiful they've seen.

After the children leave, she looks out of her classroom window and sees the ugliness of the neighborhood—the dirty streets, the ramshackle buildings, the ragged homeless people—and she feels bad for the children and thinks perhaps she's given them an assignment they can't really do. "How will they find something beautiful in this awful area?" she thinks to herself. And she worries that evening and the next morning that she has done the wrong thing.

But the next morning, when class begins and she asks the children whether any of them have seen something beautiful, she is surprised when all the children raise their hands. She calls on them one by one, and in the book, there is a beautiful painting on every page, showing the beautiful thing each child reports. One tells of the bright, pretty colors of the clothes his mother has hung up to dry on the clothesline between the tall, dirty apartment buildings. Another saw a small flower growing out of a crack in the pavement. A third saw the sun shining on his mother's face as she was preparing the table for their Sabbath meal.

I like to think that, on any given day, if a teacher were to ask me if I have seen the sunrise that morning or any other beautiful thing—for any blessing is a thing of beauty—I will always be able to raise my hand. And I wish the same for you.

· 7 ·
People Make Time for What's Important to Them

This is a truth I've discovered fairly recently, though it has some of its roots in experiences from my teenage years. The phrase came to me one evening about four years ago, when I was standing angrily at the sink in my kitchen.

I was so mad! My boyfriend and I were having a lot of arguments and disagreements, and I thought the reasons for them were mostly his fault. I wanted to spend more time together, do more fun and frivolous things like going for walks and playing miniature golf and cuddling up while watching movies. He wanted to be more spontaneous, do things when they occurred to us, not plan time for them; he wanted to spend more evenings alone at home, working on his bills, searching the Internet for information on the post-9/11 political situation, and playing his guitar. He kept saying our relationship was important to him, but he didn't want to be together more than once or twice a week. I wanted to be together a lot more than that.

One evening during this period, I was doing the dishes in my apartment, and I was sort of banging around and slamming pots and pans and grouching to myself about how mad I was.

"If he really cared about this relationship, if it was really important to him, he'd *make* time for it."

At first, when I said it aloud, it hit me hard and just made me madder and more hurt. Yep, that's really true. People make time for what's important to them. When people say, "I don't have time for that," it really means, "That is not as important to me as the things I'm already doing." He's not making time for me, for us, so our relationship isn't a priority for him. I felt worse than ever; hurt that if this was true, I wasn't really very important to him.

And then, a light bulb seemed to flicker on; and the thought that came into my mind was, if it's true for him and true for people in general, it must be true for me, too. Yikes. That simple realization made me look at myself and my own choices. What was *I* doing? What was *I* making time for? I was choosing to be mad, and I was not doing anything fun because I didn't want to do it by myself, and I was waiting around by the phone not getting anything done.

When I asked myself what was important to me, as demonstrated by what I was making time for, it seemed ridiculous: Apparently, what was important to me was feeling hurt and angry and self-righteous, was waiting for someone else to take the initiative, and holding onto my hurt and angry feelings as if they themselves had some innate value or worth.

that simple realization made me look at myself and my own choices. what was i doing? what was i making time for?

Now, it's true that this situation wasn't all about me. My boyfriend's actions *were* having some impact on it, and some of the conflict was simply about having different needs for togetherness, but I saw then very clearly that I had a part in it. I was very interested in this, and curiously, it made my feelings subside. I switched modes and started thinking about what was important to me. Shaking the soap suds from my hands, I dried them on a towel, found a pen, and wrote on a piece of paper PEOPLE MAKE TIME FOR WHAT'S IMPORTANT TO THEM. Then I stuck it on the refrigerator with a magnet.

And over the next hours and days and weeks, I spent a lot of time staring at the wall and thinking about that, and, in scattered little moments, experimenting with ways to use my time. I sought out my somewhat neglected friends and made a point of doing fun things with them; I realized I hadn't played the piano in weeks and got out my practice books; I let the housework go a little (that's a recurring theme for me ☺) and spent more time reading and relaxing and watching funny movies.

Ask Death the Question

I wasn't instantly "cured," I have to tell you. I found over those weeks that at many times, it was very hard to decide what it was I wanted to do. And I figured out that part of the reason for that was the word "important." I was having trouble deciding what to do because I wasn't clear about what was *worth* doing. Sometimes I was feeling good about my activities, but some days and nights I was in a funk of meaninglessness, and sick with the idea that nothing I did mattered.

An unexpected memory helped me shift out of that place. I was riding in my friend Terri's car, on our way to a Sunday morning breakfast at a restaurant, and as we traveled the freeway, a merging driver almost merged right into us. After Terri finished cursing him and our heart rates quieted, she said, "Oh, I wish everyone had taken a driver's education class like the one we had; remember? We learned that it's up to the merging driver to fit in with the flow of freeway traffic, and that guy wasn't doing that at all!"

I did remember that class—we were juniors in high school, and I was 15 then. As we drove along, I let my mind drift back to it: the classroom work, the funny experiences with the driving-simulator machines, the nervousness of driving with the instructor right beside you. Then I remembered that one day in the classroom, when we were learning about crash statistics and hearing a lecture about being careful drivers, the teacher had suddenly and starkly brought home to us the whole foreign, unimaginable idea of the real danger of getting killed in a car crash: He asked us to take out our notebooks, imagine that we had gotten into a fatal car accident because we weren't being careful, and then write down all the people who would come to our funeral. He gave us five minutes to work on it.

I've told a number of people about this exercise, and nobody I've met had a similar experience. Strange as it sounds, though, it was significant to me; obviously, since I've remembered it all this time.

My first thought at the time, in my then-current angst about not being popular or having very many friends, was, "Oh, probably no one would even *want* to come to it." But then I thought, "Well, even though my parents and I are always fighting, I guess they would be there . . . and probably my sister and brothers . . . and maybe my new friends at the bowling alley would come, if they heard about it in time . . . and some of the neighbors, like the couple I babysat for . . . " Well, it turned out I could come up with quite a long list.

My point here is not about traffic safety or funerals, however! The thing is, to learn about life in general, it is sometimes helpful to think about death in general. And when you're trying to learn about your own life, it is sometimes helpful to imagine your own death.

The idea of death may seem far away from you, something that happens to older people or to sick people or even to bad people. But take a minute to imagine: What if you *were* to die next week? What would your obituary say? Who would remember you? Who would miss you? Why? What would you want written on your tombstone?

What would you want to do in the next few days? What would you regret not having done?

See how it fits in here? Sometimes thinking a little about death and its inevitability helps me get clear about what's important to me in my *life*. It helps guide the choices I make about how I live. I used it when I was finishing high school and trying to figure out what to do next, and I've thought about it at a number of other times during my life, too.

As a teenager trying to figure out what was right for me, it was easier to look around at the choices people made and think of the ones I *didn't* want to make: I didn't want to get married and start having children at a young age; I didn't want to work in business or just for the money; I didn't want to be a person who worked all day and came home every night to watch TV; I didn't have the ambition to be rich or famous or powerful. I realize that those things are important to some people, but they aren't the right paths for me.

I did want to have more happiness in my life; I did want to be remembered as a good person, a wise person, someone who left the world a better place than the one she was born into; I wanted to use my talents and abilities as much as possible, to develop whatever potentials I had. I wanted to experience as much of the wonder and variety of our world as I could. I wanted to find my own voice and to be heard; I wanted to do something about the wrongs I saw in the world: mistreatment of animals and of people; industries polluting our water, our air, and our soil; discrimination against women and against minorities; the way leaders of countries go to war rather than finding more creative ways to deal with conflict.

Coming to realize what I wanted and didn't want, in that context, has helped me many times over the years to make decisions about what is worth doing and what is not worth doing, about what is important to me. There have been times when what seemed the most important thing to me was to learn as much as I could and to get good grades and to graduate—and sometimes to have as much extreme fun as possible without getting into any trouble. At other times, what has been most important is working at art and writing and music, to express my thoughts and ideas in poetry and in photography and in songwriting.

While I've worked at some jobs strictly for the money, when I was in debt or simply trying to pay my rent and buy food in a city I'd just moved to, for the most part I've looked for and have been lucky to find jobs that let me feel that my work matters more than just providing me with a paycheck. I've worked at art museums and colleges, and I work now for a nonprofit organization that combines research and community activism in trying to make the world a better place for children and youth.

sometimes thinking about death helps me get clear about what's important in my life.

Some of this certainly was triggered by that question from driver's education class about my funeral, but more important were the examples set by my parents and other family members of trying to live good lives and do meaningful work; the experiences of the satisfaction to be had from working for a cause (like volunteering on a political campaign at age 13) and helping other people; and the teachings from two books that I discovered as a teenager.

What Does It All Mean?

When I was growing up, my family was reasonably well off; we had a comfortable house to live in, a car, plenty of food to eat, decent clothes to wear. We didn't have a lot of spare money, though; the food was usually plain and simple, we had one black-and-white TV, and the clothes were homemade or bought at big yearly sales at discount prices. The one thing we had in abundance, however, was books.

Each bedroom had at least one bookcase, and in the living room, one wall was filled with floor-to-ceiling bookcases. Books were piled on the coffee table and stacked up on our bedside tables and on the floors of our rooms.

I remember one day when I was a teenager and was both bored and in a seeking mood. I climbed up on one of the big chairs in the living room, stepped over to the ledge of one of the floor-to-ceiling bookcases, and started browsing the very top shelves to see whether some book there would catch my interest.

When I think back on it now, I couldn't tell you exactly how old I was or where my parents were or what kind of a day it was. All I remember is the slightly risky feeling of stepping over to the ledge and holding on to a shelf with one hand while I pulled out book after book with the other, the certain knowledge that if my parents came in they would yell at me for doing this in such a dangerous way, the strange feeling of my hair brushing up against the ceiling . . . and the names and authors of the two books I eventually chose that day.

I wouldn't have lived my life as well as I have so far, and I wouldn't have written this book, if I hadn't read them and re-read them over the years. The philosophies contained in these two books struck me like a piercing winter wind—blowing through me and making me shiver. They forever changed the way I looked at and thought about how to live.

One is *Man's Search for Meaning* by Viktor E. Frankl. The other is *Doctor Hudson's Secret Journal* by Lloyd C. Douglas. If I were to be marooned on a desert island and could bring with me only one book, I would be completely torn about which to choose, but I know that it would come down to these two.

Viktor Frankl was a German-Jewish psychiatrist and psycho-therapist who, in 1942, along with his wife and thousands of their fellow Jews, was wrenched by the Nazis from his home, his work, and his life, and was confined for several years in concentration camps, including the infamous Auschwitz and Dachau. There he was starved, frozen, worked almost to death, and beaten. There he was not Dr. Frankl; he was Number 119,104. On his first evening in camp, when he asked another prisoner where one of his friends had been sent, the response was a hand pointing to a crematorium chimney sending a column of flame and smoke into the sky.

two books forever changed the way i look at how to live.

In this book he tells of his experiences in the concentration camps: of the selections of people to live or die; of the watery soup and crumbs of bread; of the sadistic guards and the torturing officers; of bare feet in snow on work details; of nine skinny men crowded into a single bunk bed with two blankets between them.

The historical facts he relates are enough to grab one's attention and set the reader to pondering the awful things humans do, the horrors of war, and the amazing fact that any of the prisoners survived. But what deepens his story and gives it the strength to last many years past his lifetime is the wisdom about how to live that is woven into his tales. As hard as it might be to imagine, he didn't just endure; he was actually able to find a way to make his time in captivity meaningful. After he was liberated from the final camp in 1945, he developed his own "therapeutic doctrine" about finding meaning in life, which he named logotherapy. The second half of his book explains logotherapy and how a person can use its ideas.

How to explain this book's impact on me? For one thing, to read of the true sufferings of Frankl and the other prisoners made my own dissatisfactions with my life—the difficulties of high school cliques and not being on the gymnastics team, the disappointments of disrupted friendships and boyfriends who changed their minds, of never having the "right" clothes or the "right" shoes or the "right" look, my utter lack of a clue about what I wanted to do when I graduated—melted into insignificance. After all, compared to them, what did I really have to complain about?

More intense, though, was discovering myself to be a member of the human race—realizing that just like me, many, many other people in the past and present struggled with this existential question of how to make meaning of one's life, of how we know that our life matters. For in Frankl's opinion, that is in fact the fundamental question that faces each of us. What gave his answers weight in my mind was how in the prison camps he had discovered a way to find meaning in his life even in the midst of terrible suffering: through the observation of a beautiful sunset, even though the view was through a barbed-wire fence; through giving comfort and help to the men around him; through private memories of his wife, whom he loved very much and who he later discovered had died in one of the camps; through his imagining of a future time when he would be able to write about his experiences; and through his faith and his curiosity about human nature even in the direst of circumstances.

I took that idea to heart and have held it there all these years, and when I discover that my life is feeling empty or insignificant, I often search the bookshelves for Frankl's book. When I read it, I find my way again. He reminds me that although the meaning of my life may change, there are always things that are important, that I can appreciate, that I can do for others and myself. And he reminds me that each of us has unique tasks in the world as well as the special opportunities to carry them out.

The Secret of the Secret Journal

Were you ever a Boy Scout or a Girl Scout? I was never in Scouts myself, but when I was kid, I remember that one of the ideas of Scouting, according to my friends, was to do one good deed each day, because that was the good and right way to behave. And each time there was a meeting, all the Scouts had to report what good deeds they had done.

I took the idea pretty seriously when I heard about it as a young girl, and I still do. I find it an excellent way to remind myself, on a daily basis, that my life can be meaningful and significant in the bigger scheme of things. Unfortunately, I can't tell you here about the specific things I do, because I believe, as I learned from the book *Doctor Hudson's Secret Journal,* that telling others about good deeds lessens their power for good in my own life.

This novel from the 1930s is presented in the form of a man's journal, written in code. This man, Dr. Hudson, is a brain surgeon. He chooses to write about his life in code for two reasons: one, because he doesn't want anyone to read it who hasn't at least got the strong interest and imagination to decode it; and two, because he's concerned that "normal" people, when they read it, may think that the strange events he experienced mean he is either crazy, or stupidly superstitious, or both.

Hudson has, he says, learned the secret of gaining "personal power," of becoming able to have whatever you truly want in life. It began with a seemingly chance encounter with an eccentric sculptor at the business where Hudson went to purchase a small gravestone for his late wife's grave. The artist, Randolph, claims to have found the formula in an ancient holy book. He says that all it takes to gain that power is to follow the rules: 1) to watch quietly for an opportunity to help another person, 2) to do so with humility, respect, and creativity, 3) to keep your action a secret and ask the other person to do that, too (so secretly that your own left hand doesn't know what your right hand is doing), and 4) then to wait for the invisible, inner reward of personal power.

Randolph then tells of his own experiments with this idea, relating as an example how he helped a man who was down on his luck, putting time and money that he could hardly spare into helping him get some new clothes and find a job, swearing both of them to secrecy, and how, after a successful experience, he felt more fully alive and energetic than ever before, somehow in touch with a quiet, mysterious power that made it easier for him to achieve his goals and do his best in whatever he tried to do.

Doctor Hudson's Secret Journal, in a way, takes the idea of doing good deeds and deepens it, explains it, expands it, and makes clear just exactly why that is a good thing to do. It also includes a caution: This is powerful stuff, so be careful; it could wind up changing your life. (If you want to read more about it, you can usually find a copy of the book and others by Douglas at used bookstores; it was a bestseller in its day and hundreds of thousands of copies were printed.)

I can't tell you the details of the experiments I have made. Let's just say that the experiments can be small or large, from simple acts of helping someone in momentary need to larger commitments over a long time. But I can tell you that they have made it clear to me that the most important rewards are not the external ones of money and rank and possessions, but the internal ones of peace and personal power, of satisfaction and integrity and joy in helping others realize their own potential.

The books I've described are just two examples that have influenced my own view of the world. You may have read other life-changing books, or those books may still be waiting somewhere for you—if not on a hidden top shelf in your home, perhaps in a public library or even on a table in a dentist's waiting room.

What Is Really Worth Doing?

When my father was very sick and in the hospital before he died, we had a long talk one afternoon, and I had the chance to reflect with him very specifically on the kinds of choices I was facing in my life about my work, my marriage, and my purpose. I told him I wasn't sure about any of those things and was struggling with what was important to do.

He was 77 years old at the time and had spent many years as a professor. I had always assumed that those years of teaching had been satisfying and important to him. During our discussion, he reminded me of two other jobs he had held: During World War II, he worked as a chemist making explosives. When the war ended, he went to Germany and worked for two years for his older brother. His brother, Howard, had been the head of Lutheran World Relief there, and together they did everything they could to help concentration camp survivors, released prisoners of war, and other displaced persons, as they were called, try to get back to some sort of normal life. After recounting some of the experiences he had during that time, he surprised me by saying, "Those two years were the only time in my life that I was absolutely sure that what I was doing was worthwhile."

Only two years, despite a long career committed to helping challenge, nurture, and educate young adults.

I took away from that conversation three things: reassurance, guidance, and a challenge. It was reassuring to me that even someone like my dad could wonder about what he was doing and whether he was making the right choices, and that my struggles were normal, rather than failures. In the years since then, I've seen that we can rarely know for sure the outcomes of what we do. I've come to believe that all I can do is do my best with what I've been given and trust that good is sometimes part of the end result. I try to give without thought of getting anything back, freely, without expectation.

The guidance I received that day was clear. The way I say it to myself is: "You can make a positive difference in the world, and that's just about the only thing that's really worthwhile." Now, that is not to say that I'm some sort of saint going around doing good all the time. For one thing, it takes a fair amount of time to just take care of myself, because work and the world are hard and tiring at times, and I need to relax and regain my balance periodically. Taking care of myself is worth doing, though, because when I'm strong and centered and rested and calm, I'm better at doing all the other things I think are worth doing—including having fun.

But I have taken that as the guiding principle of my life: trying to make a positive difference in the world. Each of us can find our own ways to do this. For myself, the opportunities to do so appear everywhere when I look for them, and in many different ways. I have seen how simple it is to intentionally notice how the people around me are doing at work, and to try to offer a word of understanding or empathy or encouragement. I have volunteered to help organizations whose causes I believe in,

it was reassuring to me that my struggles were normal, rather than failures.

especially ones that focus on the environment and overpopulation. I continue to watch for opportunities to do "good deeds," and I believe that has made a difference in my ability to succeed in my job and in my endeavors as a writer and singer.

The challenge I took away came from a kind of sadness I felt when Dad told me that he was only sure about those 2 years out of his 77 years of life. It was wonderful that he had done that work in Germany, but I decided I wanted to do everything I could to not end up on my own deathbed that way; I want to reach the end of my own life, whenever that may be, with more sureness about my life being worthwhile.

I want to be able to honestly say that I experienced as much of the joy and beauty of the world as I could. To do that, I seek the small joys and beauties in my daily life, and I save my money for taking occasional trips to amazing natural places like the wilderness of the Black Hills and the desert of southern Arizona.

I want to be able to say that I became more and more myself over my lifetime, that I developed my potentials, that I found my own voice and claimed my own strengths and interests. To do that, I have practiced writing and am now writing this book; when I see an injustice, I try to speak up about it; I have conquered my fears and shown others my poetry and played my own songs for them; and I renew each year my search for new interests and new ways to learn.

I want to be able to say that when I saw things that were wrong in the world, I did what I could to fight against the wrong and contribute to the good. I make sure I vote in every election. I have tried in my own ways to let the peace I want to see in the world begin with me. In all these circumstances, I have found that the comfort and strength I offer to others and to the world have become my own comfort and strength. And when you focus your time on what's truly important to you, you will find unexpected rewards like those coming your way, too.

· 8 ·
If You Want to Be Happy, Find What You Love to Do

My family was lucky: my grandpa hadn't been very well off, but he had saved his money and bought land when it was cheap, back in the 1940s, along the shore of Lake Superior, the largest freshwater lake, in terms of surface area, in the world. It's a beautiful place, with pine and birch woods, a rocky shoreline, and a little cabin looking out on the water.

When we were kids, my brothers and sister and I could roam up and down the shore a long ways. At first, there weren't any other cabins nearby, but gradually other people started building up there. One family was the Bothwells. They bought two lots, about the length of a football field away from us. They built a family cabin on one, and the oldest son, Tom, who was just finished with college, began to build his own house on the other.

I was about 13 or 14 when he started; my older brother was 15 and the other two were younger than me. We really thought Tom was cool; he was grown-up, but still young enough to seem more like us than like most adults; he had long hair and a beard and wore jeans (okay, and I thought he was amazingly cute, too, but that's not really important to the story ☺).

Tom was so nice to us; even though he was in his twenties, he talked with us as if we were grown-ups, too, and let us help with some of his tasks. We got to pick out pretty rocks to put into the mantelpiece for the stone chimney. When he was done working for the day, he'd let us join him in the one little room with a roof over it, and we'd listen to the radio and talk.

I remember asking him once if he was going to live in this house. And he said, no, he was going to sell it when it was done. I was so surprised! How could anyone put so much work into building a beautiful house like this, in this scenic place, and then not want to live there?

But he told me that he had majored in biology in college, that he was planning to sell the house to make a profit, and that he would then use that money to finance his big dream: going to live in Africa to study lions.

Now that was a dream I could relate to, in a way. I loved animals, especially my cat, and I really liked big cats, too. I remember thinking, Wow, that sounds fantastic! But it also sounded kind of unreal. When I was hiking back to our cabin over the rocks, I remember feeling very awake with a kind of wonderment, thinking, "Can a person just *do* that?! Have a dream and then make it happen, make the dream come true?"

Coming Full Circle

Now, fast-forward 20 years from that hopeful moment. I'm sitting alone in my apartment on the top floor of a big old house in Minneapolis. It's such a hot summer and I'm so depressed about the end of my marriage several weeks before that I can't eat anything except raspberry chocolate-chip ice cream. My counselor and my friends are trying to help me by telling me to focus on my new freedom to do whatever I want to do, but I can't figure out what that is. I can't, quite honestly, think of anything but feeling sad and lonely and whether I have enough ice cream left for supper.

Somewhere in my memory, though, I had stored that conversation with Tom, because suddenly, as I stared into the freezer, my mind took me back to when I was a teenager up at the lake, and I thought of Tom. I wished he was there to talk to. I recalled the fun we had, and how accepting he was of us kids, and I remembered his dream about the lions and wondered if he had really done it, really gone to Africa and made his dream come true.

Later that evening, as I was finally turning on the air conditioner, I remembered, out of the blue, one thing I had wanted to do for years: go to Hawaii to study dolphins. How could I have forgotten?

I had first heard of Earthwatch when my high school best friend, Lori, had gone on an archaeology trip organized by them. Earthwatch is a nonprofit organization that helps people who are interested in animals, other cultures, archaeology, or the environment to take educational trips all over the world. These trips take them to places where they can volunteer to help scientists in their research projects, and in the process have unique, fascinating experiences they'd never be able to have otherwise (check it out at earthwatch.org).

I remembered that before I was married, they had listed in their catalog a trip focused on studying dolphin intelligence; maybe they still offered that trip and I could go! Quickly, before I could forget or lose my courage, I turned on the computer and went on the Internet. Without much trouble, I found their site and discovered that they still offered that trip. The study was a long-term one and it was still going on with four captive dolphins in a marine mammal research lab in Honolulu, Hawaii.

As I thought more about it, I got kind of excited for the first time in ages. And soon, I decided to go for it. I would use part of a chunk of money from when my ex and I sold our house. It was ten thousand dollars, and I'd never had so much all at once. I thought that probably a financial planner—or my parents—would say, "Don't spend any of it; put it into your retirement fund or into a new house as a good investment."

can a person really just have a dream and then make it come true?!

But I have my own ideas about money and retirement and living. I decided to go halves on it. Half of it I would save—for a house someday, or for emergencies, or to invest later. The other half I would spend; a quarter of it I had already used to buy a computer, because I needed one. And the other quarter I would use for an adventure—to go be with dolphins. I scheduled the trip for January, and having that to look forward to helped carry me through the next months.

I can hardly begin to describe how wonderful it was. Yes, it was kind of hard to travel so far (the long plane ride was very uncomfortable), it was strange to stay in a dormitory and sleep in a room with my mom (I had invited her to join my adventure) and two women we didn't know. And there was so much to learn we spent every evening of that week studying dolphin anatomy and behavior as well as the sign language the dolphins had been taught.

But, oh, what an experience! The lab was right on the beach, in sight of Diamond Head and a short walk from Waikiki Beach. Unfortunately for the islands but fortunately for us, Hawaii was experiencing a drought. We had nothing but 80s, sunshine, and blue sky for the entire time we were there.

We spent all our long days seeing and hearing the dolphins and interacting with them through the tank windows. (We didn't swim with them, because they are very susceptible in captivity to human illnesses.) But four times during the week, each of us got to spend an hour or so on one of the ledges by a tank, solo with just one trainer and one dolphin, and spend that whole hour putting our sign language to use and practicing interacting with a dolphin up close.

To simply *be* with the dolphins was what was truly amazing. To touch them and feel the rubbery wetness of their skin. To learn the signs they had been taught, and then stand next to the tank to make those signs and have the dolphins understand—to really be able to talk with these animals! To have repeated sessions with one dolphin, Akeakamai, and to get to know her. To feel the excited joy of her leaping from the water to touch my outstretched arms with her pectoral fins, to be able in our last session to feel the way she leaned into my arms for a hug, and how she clicked her happiness into my ear. I walked away from that last session with such joy in my heart and mind I could barely contain it inside my skin; I felt as if I could explode with all the emotion and energy that was inside of me. And the love. The love of the dolphins, and the love of life, that it could offer such experiences.

Happiness Is the Side Effect

I can't imagine what the writers of the Declaration of Independence were thinking when they said we should all have the right to life, liberty, and the pursuit of happiness. Life and liberty, yes. But the pursuit of happiness? As if happiness is something you can chase and catch? I think that one phrase has caused a lot of trouble, and still causes a lot of trouble, for Americans.

Why? Because pursuing happiness (or any other feeling, really) is like chasing a ghost. Think of how it is with love; you can't just choose a person and decide to feel love for her or him. Instead, you might meet a specific person, get to know that person, spend time together, and share thoughts and activities. Then, maybe, love comes. Even in cases of "love at first sight," the feelings come from the connection between two people, not from the decision or desire to fall in love. If you try to take a shortcut to love by choosing the person first, you wind up in an artificial situation that is very unlikely to work out (as demonstrated by so many of the failed "reality show" romances).

It's the same with true happiness; you can't go straight to it. Instead, you have to find what you love to do, and then happiness comes as the side effect. I didn't go to Hawaii to be happy; I went to Hawaii to be with dolphins.

When I have felt the greatest joy in my life, it has come when happiness was not my goal, but when something else was my goal. When I was with the dolphins, my focus was to be present with them, to learn as much as I could about how to communicate with them, to have a new, interesting experience. I thought I might really like it, but I didn't know. I followed my interest and worked at it and learned and tried. I stopped thinking so much about what I thought was wrong with my life, and starting focusing on what was going on around me and doing my best at something that was important to me . . . and happiness came.

pursuing happiness is like chasing a ghost.

This is a hard-won truth, a hard lesson for me to learn. When I have felt the greatest emptiness, disappointment, and frustration, it has often been because of chasing happiness itself. I have sometimes used (and abused) alcohol and other drugs, stimulants and depressants, which give a kind of artificial happiness for a short time. That's often why people keep doing drugs or getting drunk again and again; they're using substances either to stop feeling pain or to make false happiness in their brains, taking what seems to be a shortcut but turns out to be a completely wrong direction. I've experienced the hangovers, the morning-after realizations ("Oh, I can't believe I *did* that!"), and the low, low feelings that usually follow those bouts of artificial happy. I wish now I'd taken the hint a lot sooner; but I was well into my twenties before I really got that stuff under control, and I've had some relapses at difficult times in my life.

But I've also had enough experiences of true happiness as the side effect of following my true interests (and sometimes by having to be brave enough to try those new things) that I trust in them now. Now I don't often seek the feeling, I usually seek *experiences*, big and small, that *lead to* the feeling.

Infinite Variety

Some of the happiest people I've met lately are the repairmen I've had come to my house. And some of the times of quiet happiness I've had during the two years I've owned my house have had to do with repairs, either having them done or doing them myself.

Who would have thought that a clothes dryer that didn't heat, a backed-up floor drain, and a broken kitchen sink drainpipe would teach me lessons in happiness?

At first I thought it was a fluke. The floor drain in the basement stopped draining after I'd been in the house for only a week or two. I wasn't pleased; how could something break so soon? But I had to deal with it. I looked in the phone book under plumbing and saw the ad for Roto-Rooter®, so I called them up. The woman on the phone was really friendly and helpful, which was good, because I had no idea, really, how to take care of house repairs! We made an appointment for the next day.

When the repair guy arrived, he said hello and headed down to the basement with his toolbox and his hanging light. I was feeling nervous and a little upset because I was afraid it was going to cost a lot and I didn't know anything about drains. I asked him if he minded whether I hung around while he worked so I could learn something about it. He glanced up at me surprised (he was lying on the laundry-room floor by this time), and smiled.

"Sure."

Then he started to explain what he was doing and it was my turn to be surprised; I actually found myself getting interested in it. He showed me what was wrong (a kind of floater ball that is supposed to rise and fall with the water level had broken and gotten wedged into the drain opening), and I found myself experiencing a little feeling of happiness about it, and he obviously did, too.

So as he worked to fix it, I asked him about his job, because he seemed to be enjoying it. "Oh, I really like it," he told me. "I get to work with my hands, I get to help fix other people's problems, and I don't have a boss hanging over me all the time."

I thought that was neat, that he'd found what he liked to do and figured out a way to make a living at it. It turned out to be the same for the other repair guys I've had over. (They have all been men, as it happens.) Each one, when I've asked, has talked about the freedom of the work, the independence of it, how they like to meet the different people they work for, how they learned it through working with older guys (sometimes their dads or uncles) who had a lot of experience, how they liked not having to work in an office or get dressed up in uncomfortable suits. Each of them, in his own way, has found that when he does a good job at the things he likes to do, a quiet sort of happiness follows.

Now, I've chosen a different kind of work. Being an editor is about making books, helping other people do their very best as writers, and managing all the different aspects of how you take written words and make a physical book out of them. I got into it right after college, after I had realized that one of the things I liked best of all was reading and writing. How cool, I thought, that if

I became an editor, companies and organizations would pay me to do what I love. I haven't always enjoyed every aspect of the specific jobs, but I like the variety of my work and how I get to keep learning about new topics.

There are all kinds of choices out there for what you can do with your life, and some of the greatest happiness can come from the satisfaction of work (paid or volunteer) you really love to do. The repair guys I met wanted to work with their hands and didn't want to go to college, and didn't need to go to college to learn their jobs. Instead, they had apprenticeships or they went to technical school to learn their trade. I went to college because I loved to learn and read, and in the process I discovered there were jobs I could do that paid me to learn and read. What I think the repair guys and I have in common is that we looked for the activities we liked to do and the talents we seemed to have, and then went looking for jobs that paid us to do those activities and develop those talents.

How Do You Do It?

The question of what you are supposed to do with your life can seem like such a big, weighty one. When I was in high school and college, the guidance counselors all seemed to want me to choose just one thing to study or specialize in, once and for all, as if there were just one thing I was meant to do and it was kind of a contest to figure it out.

Some people do seem to know early in life that they want to be a doctor, or a pilot, or a parent. They go after that in a single-minded way and that's what they become. But it didn't work out that way for me. Personally, I didn't think very hard about what I wanted to be when I grew up until I was in college and realized I'd better think of a way to make a living! I mean, I sort of knew that all kinds of people did all kinds of things, but I didn't really have a personal drive to figure it out or to do any one thing—except that I loved to read.

When I was in grade school, I got hooked on reading biographies of interesting people, lots of them (I think a big part of the appeal was the pretty red covers on the series of books on the library shelf); I loved reading about how people became nurses or major-league baseball players or chemists or leaders. Later on, in high school, we had assignments to read about all the kinds of jobs and occupations there are out there, but nothing seemed to leap out as "the right thing" for me.

When I went to college, I tried all kinds of subjects, from history to world religions to art and music to math and biology. I majored for a while in French and Political Science, then I switched to History, then to Art; I thought they were all interesting in some ways, but I just couldn't decide. Then when I discovered journalism, I realized I had found a kind of job that let me read and write about all kinds of things. I've been a reporter, a writer, and an editor ever since.

When I look back now, though, I wonder if I really looked into the possibilities enough; I know now that I might have really enjoyed making wildlife documentaries, or being a veterinarian. I might have really enjoyed a job that let me be outside more, like being a park ranger or a rancher. I've discovered all kinds of new interests, too, as I've lived my life, interests I never even knew I had or could develop!

But I've also discovered that whether you're a young person just beginning to explore jobs and interests or you're a grown-up who is already working, the basic answer to "How do you find what you love to do?" is the same: You seek out possibilities, and then you try them. Simple, right?

Well, maybe not. If you're a person who has had a strong, clear dream of what you want to be or do for work, you may be primarily occupied with figuring out how to get there. For most of us, though, it's not that simple; we don't even know where "there" is! We try things and don't like them. Or we can't seem to figure out what there is to try. Or we like so many things that it's hard to choose just one or two to do. It's confusing and frustrating.

So how do you find out about the possibilities? One way is to explore on your own (by reading, by job-shadowing someone, by checking out the programs and classes and clubs at schools, community centers, and libraries). Another way is to ask the interesting adults you know—librarians, parents, aunts and uncles, teachers, your boss. They may have ideas for you or know about interesting opportunities that you were unaware of.

One of my favorite examples of how this can work comes from my coworker, Nancy, who is the mother of two boys. When her two sons were going through their early teen years and struggling with the question of what to do, when they were getting caught in the traps of boredom, or too much TV and video games, or starting to hang out with kids who were experimenting with alcohol and other drugs, she decided to do something to help them explore their own interests. She looked and looked in catalogs and newspapers and community education classes, and she told her sons about the many different kinds of things that they could do. Then she let them each pick an unusual, interesting thing to try.

One of them, David, decided to try a class on glassblowing and really liked it. He wound up in an apprenticeship with a master glassblower. He learned to take a glob of melted sand, heat it over a very hot fire, blow through a tube and shape the glob—with hand tools, tweezers, even wet newspaper—into a sparkling, multicolored glass or fish sculpture or vase. Nancy displays the many things he's made on lighted shelves in her office. They are beautiful, and he made them himself.

Her other son, Michael, wanted something more exciting, more physical, that involved more people. She showed him a lot of possibilities, and what he picked was to become part of the Circus Juventas—a young person's circus. He became an acrobat, a high-flying trapeze artist! Wow! Nancy worries about him some, because it's a bit dangerous, but that's part of what Michael likes about it—the adrenaline rush, the excitement, and the skills he's developing.

Another way I've discovered new interests is to purposely say yes to invitations to do things I've never done before, even sometimes when they don't actually sound all that interesting to me. Just a few months ago, my friend Terri called one day to ask me to go with her to a dog show. I wasn't all that interested, even though I like animals, because I thought it would be focused on the competition and no one would let us meet their fancy, specially trained dogs, and that the whole experience would be just watching. But it was something different, I reminded myself, and so I said yes.

Turned out, we had a really good time! It was stunning to see hundreds of different kinds of dogs: big ones and little ones, curly fur and smooth fur, all different colors and shapes and faces. The competitions were like a visual feast; it's not often you get to see a dozen Great Danes or a dozen Dachshunds or a dozen Bulldogs all together in a ring, so you can compare them and notice what is typical of the breed and what is special about the individuals. And downstairs, all the owners whose competitions weren't happening yet had little areas set up, and they didn't mind at all if well-behaved attendees asked to meet their dogs. Terri and I both fell in love with a breed called Akitas, a large, muscular Japanese dog that looks like a Husky or Malamute but has lovely shadings of tans and browns and whites, and an adorable, friendly, smiling face. We were surprised when we saw a clock and found that we had been at the show for four hours; the time had flown by.

Or maybe a better way to say it is, the time had *flowed* by. One of the clues that invariably shows me that I've found a new real interest—one that can bring happiness as a side effect—is when time disappears while I'm engaged in it. That's one of the criteria for what a social scientist named Mihaly Csikszentmihalyi ("cheeks-sent-me-high"), who studies what makes people happy, calls "flow experiences." During flow experiences, everything seems to fit into place, to feel right. In addition to losing track of time, you end up with a sense of playfulness mixed with feeling in control, being very focused on what you're doing, enjoying the activity itself and not just looking forward to the outcome, and feeling competent.

So, when I want to gauge whether a new interest is one I should pursue, the best advice I give myself is: go with the flow.

What's Next?!

What I learned on my own is that there have been and will be many things over my lifetime that make me happy: from expressing myself in art or music, to contributing to the betterment of the world; from doing a job that is more physical, to doing a job that takes more of my brain; from working alone in my garden, to working with a group of people to create a series of books, to working for low pay just so I can have an experience of learning and helping.

I've been able to get past knowing what I *don't* want to do and figure out what I *do* want to do. I've been able to get past a recurring fear of not being good enough at new things. For many years, I would only try what I thought I'd be good at. What I've found, though, is that if I try something and like it, I can usually learn to be good enough at it. And if I love it, I can keep working to get better.

So what's next? I'm reading a book about Buddhism and learning about how to meditate. I'm spending more time in the evenings just playing my favorite music and dancing. I'm thinking about where else in the world I'd like to visit the next time I can take a trip. I'm choosing a day in the near future when I'm going to quit smoking for good. And I'm working every day with the knowledge that if I find what I love to do, the happiness will follow.

So what's next for *you?* Which opportunities seem the most exciting? Which past experiences are guiding your future plans? What do *you* love to do? You don't have to have all of the answers right now, but paying attention to your dreams and trying new things will help you discover throughout your lifetime the things that you love to do, too.

· 9 ·
You Can Do More Than You Think You Can

Sometimes a truth's appearance in my life is so vivid and clear, I can remember the day's weather, the physical setting, the textures and colors and smells and sounds of the occasion. This is one of those.

I was in my second year of college, 18 years old, and sitting in The Huddle, a little café in the student center. I was wearing my usual low-slung bell-bottom jeans and a T-shirt, with my hair pulled back in (and escaping from) a casual ponytail. Seated at the round, brown-Formica-topped table with me were Stephanie, an older student I didn't know, and a guy I recognized just vaguely from one of my classes.

It was evening, and not many other people were in the café. I had taken a break from studying to get some coffee and, I hoped, a little conversation. So after paying, I had looked for a table of people to join and found this one. We got acquainted a bit, and then Stephanie started talking about how she was having trouble getting enough writers for the student newspaper; turned out she was the editor. I was interested in journalism and writing and had thought of myself as becoming a writer someday, but I wasn't sure that I would be good enough and had been afraid to even try to get involved with the newspaper.

That had happened to me a lot over the years—getting stopped from even trying to do what I thought I wanted to because of fear: of failing, of looking stupid, of making a mistake in front of other people, of not being chosen, of being ridiculed or made fun of. For example, in junior high I had really, really wanted to be a cheer-leader (that's hard for me to imagine now, but it's true!), and I had practiced and practiced at home for the tryouts. But when my mom drove me over to the school and we walked up to the gym-nasium doors, and I peeked in and saw all the girls and the judges in there and heard the noise of it all, I suddenly became so afraid that I said I couldn't do it. Mom tried to encourage me, but nothing she said could get me past the surge of fear and nervousness. I made her turn around and walk away with me, and we drove home with me slumped down in the seat feeling like the biggest loser in the world.

Anyway, back to that evening in the café. I was impressed by Stephanie; she could only have been a year or two older than me, but she was actually in charge of the newspaper, and she seemed so confident, down-to-earth, and friendly as she talked with my classmate. Somehow, in a pause in their conversation, I managed to blurt out with honesty that I had wanted to try doing newspaper reporting, but that I had been too afraid. Stephanie looked at me in a very open, curious, and sort of friendly laughing way.

"Oh, just do it anyway!"

That's the moment I remember so clearly: the smooth feeling of the table under my shaking hand, the look on her face, the offhand way she dismissed fear as if you could step over it like a banana peel on the sidewalk.

"Just do it anyway."

Instantly, I trusted her, and even though I wasn't sure I could do it, I said, "Okay." Within 15 minutes, I had my first assignment as a reporter for the Augustana *Mirror* student newspaper.

I learned when I turned in that assignment about what an editor really does to help a writer be as clear, concise, accurate, and thorough as possible. Stephanie had to do a lot of revisions, but she did them in a kind, helpful way, and my next assignments were much improved as I learned the special techniques of reporting. Within a few months, I was a regular writer for the paper. Within a year, I was helping with the layout and editing of other reporters' stories and articles. And the year after that, I was the editor of the *Mirror* myself. I had found a kind of work I liked and was successful at—and I've worked with publications ever since.

I don't know whether I was born with my timidity or inadvertently raised to be that way or cursed with it as part of my sensitive nature. However it came to be, I have many strong memories of fear and self-doubt, and the tendrils of those childhood fears and doubts still reach into my life now. But thanks to Stephanie, I learned a technique for getting past the fear of doing something I really want to do: do it anyway.

I wish I'd known that strategy earlier in my life; it would have saved me from a lot of agony, I think!

I Can't Talk . . . or Can I?

One of the things we had to do at my high school to meet the requirements for graduation was to take a class in either theater or speech. I put it off as long as possible because I was so shy and afraid to talk in front of other people. Looking back, I think I probably would've enjoyed theater more than speech, because I know now that I like drama and acting. At the time, however, I made my choice out of fear. I figured it would be bad enough to have to stand up in front of other people and give a speech. Theater class, I reasoned, would be even worse, because I'd have to stand up on a stage and have everyone look at me even more. So I took speech my junior year, even though I thought I would hate it and be terrible at it.

Well, it pretty much turned out the way I thought it would. The teacher was kind of a cold fish, not very encouraging to those of us who were shy (and I was pretty sure no one else was as shy and terrified as I was). The class was very formal, and we had to learn a certain style of speaking. I don't actually remember any of the topics I spoke about, just the fear and worry and anxiety beforehand, the feeling of standing up there being utterly exposed and vulnerable, with everyone staring at me, and not even being sure what words were coming out of my mouth. I worked at it some, practicing and practicing at home and hating every minute of it. I managed to get through the class, I think with a C, and was so grateful when it was over.

When I got to college, I kept quiet in class at first, because I was still really shy. I also didn't think I had anything useful to say, or that anyone would be interested in or persuaded by it. But I got excited about some of my classes, much more so than I did in high school. I took philosophy and literature and history, and learned about ideas that seemed to physically excite my brain. I couldn't help talking about them in class sometimes. And people actually listened. Sometimes my classmates disagreed with me, and sometimes the professors pointed out that I was wrong, or that I hadn't taken all the facts into account, or that I had judged something too soon without thinking it through—but they listened, and sometimes I made good, imaginative contributions to the discussions. After a while, I grew more accustomed to and actually started to enjoy saying what was on my mind. I got so that I was comfortable talking with just about anyone one-on-one, and sometimes in a group. I was still convinced, however, that I never wanted to be up on a stage or behind a podium speaking formally to a group.

Now leap ahead 20 years. I was just beginning to work at the job I'm in now. It's an office job, working as an editor and figuring out what sorts of books and posters and workbooks my organization ought to publish. My boss told me that I needed to start to learn to make presentations at our all-staff meetings. Oh, horror! It was going to be 11th-grade speech class all over again.

i learned a technique for getting past the fear of doing something i really want to do: do it anyway.

But I had no choice; I had to "do it anyway." I was sure my voice would crack and choke, and whatever I said would sound dumb and that it would be horrible, but I had to do it. Sure enough, when I got up to the front of the room and began reading my ideas from the paper clutched tightly in my hand, my voice did shake a little bit. I couldn't even see the people in front of me; it was as if my vision wasn't working right, and all I could hear was a kind of roaring, like the sound when you put a big seashell to your ear, and I couldn't tell what I was really saying. I tried to pretend I was calm and cool, and I smiled, even though I'm pretty sure it looked phony.

But afterward, I asked one of my trusted friends how I did, and she said I did great!

"Are you kidding? I was so scared and anxious, and I couldn't tell what I was saying, even."

"Seriously?" she asked. "Well, I couldn't tell from the outside."

Apparently, my put-on confidence was effective. I was so relieved! My face didn't show that I was scared. Right then, I started to think that maybe I could learn how to do this. If I wasn't totally embarrassing myself, maybe I could actually do it. I guess I'd been imagining that people could see my fear, would see me as a scared, shaking little girl. But they didn't. And that gave me a little courage, a little freedom from my fears and doubts, a little self-confidence.

I started to try doing presentations without writing everything down and then reading it. I still felt during the talks that I didn't really know what words were coming out of my mouth, but I knew I was saying what I really thought, and when I asked people afterward, they would say it was best when I could hear myself the least. Strange but true! So I started trusting myself more, taking more opportunities to try it . . . because I no longer was so afraid that I'd have the biggest failure in the world every time I got up there.

Now I actually really like doing presentations. I call them "speeches" and tell my staff, "I'm going to give a speech today." That always makes me laugh, because it's me remembering how afraid I was in speech class so many years ago. Just a few weeks ago, I told one of my staff (I have four people who work for me now) that just five years ago, I was so shy that I couldn't talk in front of a group, and she didn't believe me. She thought I'd been born with this ability. And I was so proud of myself and so amazed. I did it. I really did it. I learned how to do something I was afraid of, and I even learned how to do it well! I had told myself "I can't," but I did it anyway and it turns out I can.

Taking Good Risks

Now, I'm not saying that all fears are to be stepped over and ignored. Fear is a signal of potential danger, and so it is a protective feature of our bodies and minds. It tells us that whatever it is we're considering doing involves some risk.

I've found I have to weigh the size and shape of the risk and weigh the size and shape of the fears, too, in order to make the good choices. I've seen that sometimes my fear is large because the risk is large (for example, when I weigh the danger of driving drunk; the danger of that is real, and that danger is the big danger of death—

my own or someone else's). But sometimes my fear is large when the real risk is small—for example, when I've been afraid to try a new sport because I'm afraid I'll make mistakes and look silly. The danger can feel big to my ego, but it is really pretty small.

And I have to weigh the possible benefits and opportunities, too. When my fears and doubts are ungrounded or are out of proportion, they can sometimes stop me from getting great benefits. If I hadn't gotten past my doubts and fears about writing for the college newspaper, I would have missed a whole career!

Sometimes people call that fluttery feeling of fear "having butterflies in your stomach." Nowadays, I love what Becky Judd (a woman in Alaska who is a great activist on behalf of young people) says about this: "Get your butterflies raging." She means that sometimes that butterflies feeling is a sign that you need to have courage to do something really interesting or important. It reminds me that just because I notice the fear doesn't automatically mean I should stop myself from doing something new.

I had a swimming teacher some years ago, for a community education class in water aerobics, who used to point at a poster on the wall if someone in the class complained that they couldn't do the exercise she had just asked us to do. The poster said, "CAN'T" IS NOT IN MY VOCABULARY.

I used to argue with her in my head, thinking that it just wasn't realistic to think that everyone could do every exercise, and it used to annoy me. Then I re-read a book I had liked in college, *Illusions: The Adventures of a Reluctant Messiah,* by Richard Bach. A slightly smart-alecky statement from that book jumped out at me and reminded me of my reaction to that poster: ARGUE FOR YOUR LIMITATIONS, AND SURE ENOUGH, THEY'RE YOURS.

I realized that when I said, "I can't," sometimes I was doing just that: arguing for my limitations. And when I argued for them, sure enough, they were mine. By choosing to limit myself and limit my activities, I was putting limits on my potential achievements. I wondered what might happen if, instead, I chose to take the attitude of "I can"—or at least the attitude of "Maybe I can."

Don't Quit Just Because It's Hard

I had a terrible phase in my first year of high school when I quit everything. I quit gymnastics because, compared to junior high, the coach was very hard-nosed and mean-sounding, and it seemed to be all about competition and winning and not at all about fun, gracefulness, and strength. I quit chorus at school. I quit choir at church. I quit playing the recorder. I quit playing the piano.

I don't mean that it's *never* okay to quit. In fact, when I look back on that time today, I think I might have been right to quit gymnastics; that coach would have made it impossible for me to do well. And I also know now that I was probably depressed; I take an antidepressant now that helps me stay on track and make better decisions. But I think I quit most of the other activities because they'd gotten too hard in some way: too much competition, too much need for practice and dedication and never having a break, challenging new levels I was expected to perform at.

It took me quite a number of years to come back from that experience, and one of the people who helped me the most was a male friend of mine. Whether we were riding bikes up a long, steep hill or hiking up a mountain or struggling to complete our first song, he didn't treat the difficulties as reasons to quit. He stayed focused on the goal, the outcome, and I internalized that idea for myself with the phrase, "It's hard but it's good."

I remember our first big wilderness hike together. We were going camping, and we both put on our big heavy backpacks so that we could hike far enough into a national park to get away from all the other people and have a good chance of seeing wildlife. I thought I had been training pretty well, with all the walks we'd been taking, but when I started taking steps with forty pounds of pack on my back, I almost overbalanced and toppled over beside the trail!

I didn't tell him out loud, but in my head, I thought, "Omigod, I don't know if I can *do* this!" But there he was, striding along the trail ahead, looking back at me.

"Come on!"

What could I do but start taking steps? We were in Organ Pipe National Monument in southern Arizona, a beautiful desert area filled with gorgeous cacti and rocks and sand the colors of the sunset. Being surrounded by that beauty, by the clear, dry desert air and the searing blue sky helped a bit. Each step was heavy; each rise in the trail taxed my strength, especially in my knees and thighs. My shoulders were sore from the weight, and after awhile all I could do was keep putting one foot in front of the other, counting 1, 2, 3, 4 to myself over and over, trying not to think about how hard it was, and letting time just slip away.

When we arrived at what looked like a good campsite, we stopped and put down our packs (finally!). We set up our tent, and he got out our stove and started cooking dinner. I took a little time to rest and stretch my sore muscles, and then I just sat for awhile, taking it all in. The sky, the air, the colors of the blooming cactus flowers, the scent of sage and stone, the light so liquid you felt you might be able to open your mouth and drink it, the view of dusky purple hills and red cliffs, and in the midst of a deep stillness, sounds of birds I'd never seen or heard before. It was wonderful, and I never could have experienced it without doing that extremely difficult hike—the one I didn't know if I could do.

He looked up from his cooking and asked me how the hike had been for me. "Hard," I replied. "Hard but good."

What One Person Can Do

Sometimes, life seems to pile up, everything seems challenging, and it feels as if we're asked to do far more things than anyone possibly can. I read the newspaper and listen to the radio, and there are just too many problems to solve. Sometimes I wind up doing nothing because of that.

I am thankful to have a good job, but sometimes the job is very hard (yes, I'm reminding myself, "hard but good"), and when I come home after a long day, there sit the dirty dishes, and the overgrown lawn, and the books piled all over the place waiting to be put back on the shelves. Then there are my bills to pay and the toilet that keeps running and needs to be fixed, and the weeds that are choking out the flowers in the back flowerbed, and this book that is waiting to be finished . . . and I think to myself, "I can't do *everything!*"

And of course that's true. None of us can do everything, but each of us can do something.

One of the stories I like to tell that illustrates this point happened to me when I was in my thirties. I had realized by then that I had been pretty lucky to get through my teenage years, and I wanted to do something real to help other people get through theirs in the best possible way. So I signed up to become a volunteer at St. Joseph's Home for Children and became part of a group of adults and teenage boys who spent time together each week. I wasn't sure of what I would have to offer these guys, all of whom were living away from their families and had run into some pretty serious difficulties in their lives. But I knew that places like that were always wanting more volunteers, and I wanted to try to help.

Before I could be part of the group, though, I had to attend a volunteer training. I felt a little nervous going to the class that Saturday morning, as I often do when I'm going to try something brand new and don't know much about it. But I was really hoping that I wasn't

I was just one person, but I had decided to act, and I discovered that doing what I could was enough to make a contribution. I keep using this truth in my life by choosing to look for the things I *can* do, even though I know I can't do everything. I can spend some of my spare time working for the candidates I think will bring good values and plans to the place where I live. I can lift one person's spirits by giving her or him a sincere compliment or offering encouragement on a tough day. I can learn to repair my own toilet, even though I've never taken any plumbing lessons. I can move beyond my unreasonable fears in order to try new activities that stretch my abilities and help me grow as a person. I can keep on building up my core of confidence, my courage, and my carefulness.

If I want it, I can find a way to make it happen—maybe not exactly the way I hoped or intended, because not everything is in my control, but a path can be found, a step can be taken on the way. Because I've proved to myself that I can do more than I ever thought I could, and it's true that you can do more than you ever thought you could, too.

· 10 ·
This, Too,
Shall Pass

I'll never forget what it was like when my dad died. I had
suffered other losses: my grandfather and grandmother when
I was still a kid, one of my friends when we were in our late teens
(motorcycle accident), my beloved cat when I was in my twenties.
But when Dad died, it was so different, so much worse. I felt it
like a storm blowing in grief and anger.

He had been sick for some time, but in recent weeks, he'd
had a hernia operation and wasn't recovering from it very well; he
wasn't regaining his basic body functions and he had emphysema
from smoking all his life. On what turned out to be the last weekend of his life, I had driven down to Sioux Falls, where my parents
still lived and where Dad was in the hospital. My mom, my siblings,
and I didn't know if he would make it, but it was starting to seem
as if he'd never get well, and we were scared and worried and upset.

I spent that weekend sitting with Dad in his hospital room,
talking with him when he was clear in his mind, just listening
sometimes when he was having what he called "daytime dreams"
of people from his past. I talked a lot with my sister, helped Mom
get some rest and some groceries, slept at home in Dad's bed with
the phone on the bedside table.

On Sunday morning, the phone rang right by my ear and jolted me awake. It was still dark. The nurse who called said Dad had taken a turn for the worse; they didn't think he'd make it through the day; we'd better come.

I woke Mom, called my sister, made a thermos of coffee to take in the car, all in a zombie-like daze of sleepiness and confusion and struggling to be in control enough to take care of Mom and drive safely. Dad was unconscious when we got there, and he never regained consciousness.

We talked to the doctors and they said all they could do was try to keep Dad comfortable. We called our brothers in the Twin Cities, several hundred miles away, and told them to come. My mom and sister and I took turns being with Dad, sometimes all of us together in his room, taking turns crying and losing the box of tissues. One of his friends came to visit, and that friend called other friends, and so we had visitors during the afternoon who talked with us about Dad and read favorite poems aloud and cried with us and held our hands.

I had to drive back to the Twin Cities in the late afternoon; I had deadlines at work that I had to take care of the next day, and there was nothing I could do for my dad. I had said goodbye, and now it was just a matter of waiting for him to die. I drove home vacillating between tears and an unreal feeling of numbness.

Monday morning was a horrible repeat of Sunday. In the pre-dawn darkness the phone rang loud and woke me up. I stumbled to it and picked up the receiver and heard my sister's voice, choked up and crying, telling me that a little while ago Dad had died.

How Do People Survive?

I hung up the phone after we agreed to talk later. I doubled over because my stomach suddenly clenched and I felt a huge sob rise up in my chest and come out as an unearthly howl of grief. Tears streamed down my face. After a little while the tears slowed, and I made and drank some coffee, took a shower and got dressed in order to go to work. I called my boss to tell her what had happened, so people at work would not be surprised to see my red eyes.

Then I picked up my keys and walked out the door, locked it, and started down the concrete steps to head for the car. Without any warning I was suddenly overwhelmed with grief again, and I stopped in my tracks at the bottom of the stairs. It was like a tidal wave of horror and sadness and it felt so big, I wasn't sure I could handle it. It felt as if it might knock me over.

Somehow, I was surprised. I had thought I knew what it was like to feel grief. I thought I understood how bad it could get. I thought I'd already been through the worst. I had experienced the deaths of people close to me; I'd struggled with depression; I'd been fired from a job; I'd had months of being unemployed; I'd had important relationships end with terrible fights and angry breakups followed by deep loneliness and self-doubt. And I'd gotten through, I'd survived all that. But I'd never known grief could be so deep, so overwhelming, so physical, so all-encompassing.

it was like a tidal wave of horror and sadness and it felt so big, i wasn't sure i could handle it.

And I thought of people who were parents and had suffered the death of a child, and of people who'd lost the use of part of their body, and of people who lived in utter poverty and in war-torn countries, people who didn't have loving parents, who even had terrible parents. I cried and cried and was consumed by the weight of all of the things that people survive or have to live through as they grow ever older.

"I didn't know, I didn't know!" I screamed in my mind. "I didn't know how bad it could be! How do people live through these things?!"

What pulled me back from the swirl of pain was the realization that people do, in fact, live through these things. Somehow, they manage to keep going, to keep living, to move forward. And in that realization, I found hope that I could get through this, too; that even though I couldn't imagine it, there must be life on the other side of this grief.

I had learned, long before, a saying from the Old Testament in the Bible: This, too, shall pass. It's an old, old idea, and one that has been common to many ancient and modern cultures. No matter how bad it gets, no matter how *good* it gets, life moves on, things change. That can be a sad thought when times are good, but a comforting one when times are bad. But what's really useful about it for me is that thinking about it helps my mind get involved in a situation of strong feeling, and then I can start using the truths I know to help me figure out what I can and should do next.

Remember Your Truths When Life Gets Hard

When I told my sister, Nancy, about this book and especially about this chapter, she said, "Yeah, but how do you *remember?* When you're feeling upset and just wanting to escape, and when it's not just one tough thing that's happening but two or three at once, how do you *remember* the truths that work for you?"

Good question. It may not work for everyone, but here's what I do.

First, I try to notice how strong my emotions are. One of the things I learned from a counselor when I was in my twenties sticks in my head:

STOP AND THINK.

Easier said than done, of course. But I know from experience that if I take the time to feel the emotions but not act on them right away, my better judgment eventually kicks in and I can *think* about what's best to do. I also know from experience that I don't always make my best decisions when I just react or respond to my emotions.

When things are very hard and upsetting, reaction can make me want to escape, want to run away, or drown my emotions in alcohol, or take my mind off the situation with other substances, or do something impulsive without thinking of the consequences. (Been there, done that, more times than I like to admit. Once after a breakup, I cut off almost all my hair, feeling that I needed to do something drastic, something on the outside that showed the change on the inside of me.)

If my emotions are really strong and I can sense the urge to react or do something drastic, I ask myself, How can I get through this time safely? How do I keep myself from doing anything rash that might have bad consequences that just make the situation worse? One of the things I do in that case is pretty simple: I stay home.

I take time alone, quiet time, to let the reasons for my feelings get clear. I might sit for an hour in a fragrant bath letting my fingers and toes get all wrinkled. I might work in my garden, just doing something mindless like pulling weeds or mowing the lawn. I might do the dishes or the laundry, chores I don't really like, but that don't take much brain power. And I let the feelings come and see if any thoughts come, too. Sometimes, I've had the experience then of having the thought surface that I'm angry and fed up and nothing works, so I might as well just get drunk or just end the relationship or just quit doing anything, extreme ideas. But since I'm safely at home, I can stop and think about those ideas. I think, Okay, I could do any of those things, but what good will that do? Does it ever solve anything if I drink, or does it just add a hangover to my problems?

Another thing that often works is to listen to my body. I lie down on the floor, maybe put on some music, and just try to be aware of where I'm tensed up. Often, that is in my stomach and shoulders and jaw. So, I think about all the parts of my body one at a time, and try to relax the ones that are tense. Usually, that helps me breathe more deeply and more regularly, which is a calming thing for everyone.

Then I listen for what my body can tell me. It might tell me I'm tired, which always makes everything worse. So if I can, I take a nap, or if it's evening, I decide that for now, the best thing I can do for the situation is sleep on it.

It might tell me I'm angry, if my hands keep clenching up into fists. It might tell me I'm afraid, if my stomach feels nervous or sick. I pay attention to it, and try to do things that help; if I'm angry I need to calm down. If I'm afraid, I need to find reassurance and comfort. If I'm hungry or thirsty, I rummage around for something to eat and drink.

If I'm somewhere where I don't want to lie down, it sometimes works just as well to simply change my body position. If I'm sitting down, I stand up; if I'm working with my hands at the computer or with some papers or books, I put them down and stretch my arms up over my head. That simple act of changing body position brings the possibility of change to my mind and emotions—it's almost like magic.

When I'm really stuck, or sometimes when I want help getting to the heart of something more quickly than I can by myself, I talk things over with someone. Usually, it's with one of my siblings, or a close, trusted friend, or a wiser, older coworker, or, especially when I'm feeling depressed, with a very good counselor. Sometimes, it helps just to be listened to; sometimes it helps me to find errors in my thinking when I talk about my feelings out loud, and sometimes the other person is able to see more clearly into the situation than I can and offer new perspectives.

If I don't feel like talking to someone or if my friends aren't available, sometimes I write about what's going on. I write fast at first, just pouring it out onto paper or into the computer so it's not stuck swirling around inside of me. And as I keep writing, I often find that it helps me figure things out. When I write, I can make new connections or realize that the conclusions I had already come to aren't very logical when I see them in black and white. Sometimes I turn what I'm writing into a letter to someone; I find that when I try to explain it to someone else, I wind up explaining some things to myself, too. By the time I'm done writing, it usually happens that by setting all the emotions and circumstances out on a page, I've cleared the confusion out of the way, and the truth I need to remember becomes visible again.

What's the Point?

If none of those activities seem to help, I try to think out of the box a little bit. Maybe I need to visit one of my friends who has a little baby and spend time with a nonverbal human; that can be incredibly soothing. Maybe I need to play some old music really loud and sing and dance with abandon in my living room. Maybe I need to ride my bike over to the park and see whether there might be a family there that will let me play outside with their kids—throw a ball, goof around on the swings, hit the tetherball, slide down the slide. (I've found that the little girl I once was still exists inside of me, in a way, and sometimes the best way to deal with having to be a grown-up is to take a little time to let that little girl just play.)

The point is to try to get myself back into balance, to get stable and centered again, so that I resist putting my weight on a moving foot. I do these things as a way of preparing myself so that my own truths will come to me; putting myself into reception mode, so that the good messages can get through the emotional static.

When I seem to be going down a path of anger or grief, I can use these things to turn myself around, to pivot away from blaming others or feeling sorry for myself. I use them to give myself the time and space to experience and process my true feelings, and once I find out what's really going on with myself, I can do something about it.

Then I can ask myself: What do I want? What do I need? What do I hope? I can look at the situation and find the parts that I might have some control over, and find the positive things I can do to take care of myself, even though in many cases I can't make the pain go away and I can't change the basic situation.

The Spiral of Life

A human life is not a straight line that you move along; it's not a single mountain you climb and reach the top of and you're done. It's a spiral, and things come around again and again, the good times and the bad times, the joys and the grief, the struggles and the victories, the same questions and difficulties at a deeper level each time you go around.

What's tricky as a teenager is that you're only on the first ring of the spiral, so not only is your brain command center still developing, but you're hitting a lot of the tough decisions and difficult situations for the *first* time, so they're not only hard, but they're very unfamiliar and strange to you, too. (On the bright side, it is dealing with these decisions and situations that helps your own command center emerge and grow strong.) You reach middle school or high school, and suddenly there are so many more students and the demands of your classes are so much greater and the cliques seem so rigid and mean, and you have to compete more, for grades, in sports, for girlfriends and boyfriends, for a good image or a good reputation, and you have new longings for love and more loneliness, maybe.

You have the stress of dealing with violence and wondering if you're going to be safe. You have to make decisions about drugs and alcohol and driving and sex and classes and jobs, and the odds are you're going to make some mistakes—maybe you already have. And then you have to deal with the consequences . . .

You have wonderful times of dating and then a breakup that feels as if it's crushing you with loneliness or battering you with anger. You have friends you're close to, and then the friendships come apart; sometimes friends even die, in accidents or through illness or by suicide, and you feel the overwhelming sadness and grief that comes with those different endings.

**a human life
is not
a single mountain
you climb and
reach the top of
and you're done.**

You see the world as a place that has not only beauty and fun in it, but also war and lies and death. You see that your parents and you and your friends and everyone else aren't perfect, that we all have our strengths and our weaknesses, our good points and our areas of need.

All these things can get you down—sometimes it's just the blues for a while, other times it's so big it lasts a long time, and sometimes this stuff can throw you into a real depression so you have trouble eating and sleeping and seeing any point in doing anything at all. You get crabby or sad or irritable or angry. You think you might as well just focus on having fun in any way you can because nothing you do will make a difference. Or you think nothing matters, you think no one cares, you feel so alone and misunderstood that you might even entertain the question of whether life is worth living.

You Are Not Alone

If ever you have the feeling of total aloneness, that no one can understand, that no one else can feel the feelings you're having, please, tell yourself this:

I AM NOT ALONE.

Because you're not. Your connection to the universe and to all the other creatures in it is there, even when you can't feel it. And you can find it again: by reaching out to someone you can trust, to a parent, a friend's parent, an aunt or uncle, a teacher, a counselor, a pastor or priest or rabbi or nun or imam, a good neighbor or a group leader at a youth program, a grandparent; by spending some time in nature; by playing with a little child or a friend; by exercising hard enough to really sweat; by reading a new book and finding out that the author has gone through things like this, too. You can seek out the stories and traditions of your own family's religion and the other belief systems and philosophies of the world. You are part of a long line of other humans, just as I am, a line that doesn't start or end with you, and the others have gone and are going through difficult things, too.

What is different as you get older, if you work at it a bit, is that you begin to know more, to have learned from your experiences, to have brought together the help you can get from the people and places around you, and so you can meet the challenges with more strength, with more ideas, with faith that you will get through one way or the other, because you have so many times before. And I believe that you'll find that life does get better, and deeper, too, when you find and trust in your own truths along the way.

What I Know So Far

Some people, as they age, wish they could be younger again, wish they could return to the time of high school or college. I sometimes wish I didn't have to face the effects of aging—it's hard to believe that stuff of creaking bones and wrinkles and middle age is actually happening to me. But I wouldn't go back for anything. I love being in my forties, because now I am getting some of the rewards for the experiences I've had since I was a teenager. Life still freaks me out sometimes, but I know I can deal with it.

- I'm more comfortable with myself than ever before—no midlife crisis for me; midlife liberation instead.
- While I have my moments of vulnerability and feeling powerless, for the most part I'm confident in my ability to learn and to succeed and to do whatever I want to do.
- Now when fears come, I recognize them much more quickly for what they are and tackle them head on. I know how to look inside myself to find courage and I know I can find help when I need it if I just look for it.
- I see my blessings, small and large, more clearly.
- I do more of what I love to do, and I'm finding new things to love all the time. I take responsibility for how I spend my time, and I value my down time and my play time just as much as my work time and my sleep time!
- I can see my strengths, accept my weaknesses, and know how to keep the embers of joy burning somewhere deep inside of me.
- I still have conflicts as well as joys in my relationships with friends and family—but I don't lose myself in them the way I used to. I'm getting better at giving freely but not giving too much, and at knowing I deserve the same

in return. And I know now what my teacher, John Eggers, meant when he said that love is nice, but it's not necessary.

◈ I've gotten into the habit of saying, "Maybe I can do that," or even sometimes, "Sure, I can do that." Why, just last week I spent a morning repairing that running toilet all by myself; I read up on it, got the right parts, had the right tools, and took the attitude of "I can do this," and sure enough, I could. Who ever thought fixing a toilet could be so much fun!?

I've also become more accepting of what Confucius said: that change is the only constant in life. I'm resistant to change at times; some changes that come don't seem to be for the better; sometimes change is gain and sometimes loss. But I've lived long enough and experienced enough to know with certainty that when one door closes, life will open more; when one relationship ends, there is loss, but there is also the freedom to become ever more myself; that my own power is mine for good, if I choose to make it so. And I believe that every day, week, and year to come will bring me new experiences to expand what I know so far.

· What I Believe ·

15 Other Great Books That Have Helped Me along the Way

I guess with one parent a teacher and the other a librarian, I couldn't have grown up *without* a love of books; I've read hundreds, maybe thousands in my lifetime so far. But the ones I've chosen here are books that have made a difference to me, changed me, taught me—books I've read over and over and learned more from each time. I wouldn't be who I am without them. I hope you'll try one of them next time you're looking for a new idea or a new companion on your journey. (The first date listed is the original publication date; the publisher and second date refer to a more recent copy that may be easier to find in print.)

- *Zen and the Art of Motorcycle Maintenance*
  by Robert M. Pirsig (1974)
  (Perennial Classics; New York, NY; 2000)

- *The Human Comedy* by William Saroyan (1943)
  (Harcourt; San Diego, CA; 1989)

- *The Road Less Traveled* by M. Scott Peck (1978)
  (Touchstone Press; Beaverton, OR; 2003)

- *The Teachings of Don Juan: A Yaqui Way of Knowledge* by Carlos Castaneda (1971) (Washington Square Press; New York, NY; 1985)

- *Lost Horizon* by James Hilton (1933) (Pocket Books; New York, NY; 1988)

- *A Wrinkle in Time* by Madeleine L'Engle (1962) (Yearling Books; New York, NY; 1973)

- *Narcissus and Goldmund* by Herman Hesse (translated into English 1971) (tr. Ursule Molinaro; Picador; New York, NY; 2003)

- *Incident at Badamya* by Dorothy Gilman (1989) (Fawcett; New York, NY; 1990)

- *The Secret Garden* by Frances Hodgson Burnett (1911) (HarperTrophy; New York, NY; 1998)

- *Out of the Silent Planet* by C.S. Lewis (1938) (Scribner; New York, NY; 2003)

- *Dibs in Search of Self* by Virginia M. Axline (1964) (Ballantine Books; New York, NY; 1986)

- *Buffalo Gals and Other Animal Presences* by Ursula K. Le Guin (1987) (Penguin Group (USA) Incorporated; New York, NY; 1994)

- *Black Like Me* by John Howard Griffin (1960) (New American Library; New York, NY; 2003)

- *Awakening the Buddha Within: Tibetan Wisdom for the Western World* by Lama Surya Das (1997) (Broadway Books; New York, NY; 1998)

Other Places to Look for Help along Your Way

For young people:

- **www.sxetc.org**—A Web site by teens, for teens, that provides information on a wide variety of sexuality topics, including body image, pregnancy prevention, and GLBT issues. The site was developed by the Network for Family Life Education through Rutgers, The State University of New Jersey.

- **www.goaskalice.com**—A health Q & A service produced through Columbia University. Readers can pose questions on any health issue, from nutrition and tattoos to drug abuse and fitness.

- **www.kidshealth.org/teen**—Offers articles on various teen health topics, including mental illness, stress management, and learning disorders. Each article is reviewed by at least one doctor, and information about all of these expert reviewers is included on the Web site.

- **www.freevibe.com**—Produced by the U.S. National Youth Anti-Drug Media Campaign, an initiative of the Office of National Drug Control Policy (ONDCP). This Web site offers facts on various drugs, alcohol, and tobacco. It also includes message boards, anti-drug e-cards, and quizzes for testing your drug knowledge.

@ **www.outproud.org**—The U.S. National Coalition for Gay, Lesbian, Bisexual & Transgender Youth. Includes coming-out stories from GLBT teens, advice on dealing with homophobia and questioning your sexuality, and a searchable Community Role Models Archive.

For parents:

@ **www.parent-teen.com**—An online magazine for parents of adolescents with a focus on offering teens straightforward information and respect.

@ *The Teen Code* by Rhett Godfrey (New York, NY: Rodale, 2004). Written by an 18-year-old, this book draws on quotes and anecdotes from more than 1,000 teens across America to help parents learn how to talk to teenagers about difficult issues.

Acknowledgments

I am so grateful:

For encouragement and comments on early drafts, from Mark Andersen; Todd, Steve, and Nancy Hong; Tom Mayer, Ree Reents, Molly McCarty, Michael McKnight, Shelby Andress, Brian Gevik, Kathy McHugh, Liz Brekke, and Nancy Tellett-Royce;

For careful review and helpful suggestions, from Aaron Wimsett, Laura Baker, David Royce, Sharon Rodine, Garland Patton, Jr., Nicte Da Casta, Lisa DeWall, Catherine Stifter, Artec Durham, David Walsh, Ruth Taswell, Betsy Gabler, Deborah Magnuson, Pat Howell-Blackmore, and my colleagues Debbie Grillo, Gene Roehlkepartain, Bill Kauffmann, Mary Ellen Buscher, Kathleen Kimball-Baker, and Anitra Budd;

For reassurance and guidance in becoming an author, from Jennifer Griffin-Wiesner;

For the idea to write this book in the first place and assistance in making it the best it could be, from Tenessa Gemelke; and

For help along the path of my life, from family, friends, and colleagues too numerous to name—you know who you are.

About the Author K.L. Hong has been a writer and editor for more than 23 years, contributing to many publications on youth and community development. Hong also has worked with young people as a volunteer at St. Joseph's Home for Children in St. Paul, Minnesota. The author received a Bachelor of Arts in English, History, and Religion from Augustana College in Sioux Falls, South Dakota. She lives in St. Paul.

About Search Institute Search Institute is an independent, nonprofit, nonsectarian organization whose mission is to provide leadership, knowledge, and resources to promote healthy children, youth, and communities. The institute collaborates with others to promote long-term organizational and cultural change that supports its mission. For a free information packet, call 800-888-7828.

About the Developmental Assets The Developmental Assets are a set of positive qualities, skills, experiences, and opportunities that help you become a strong, healthy adult. Spread across eight broad areas of human development, these assets describe the positive things all people need to grow into healthy and responsible individuals. Nobody attains all of these assets alone; you may turn to parents, teachers, friends, and other caring people as you seek these strengths in your own life.

The first four asset categories focus on external structures, relationships, and activities that create a positive environment for young people:

♥ **Support**—Young people need to be surrounded by people who love, care for, appreciate, and accept them. They need to know that they belong and that they are not alone.

☀ **Empowerment**—Young people need to feel valued and valuable. This happens when youth feel safe, when they believe that they are liked and respected, and when they contribute to their families and communities.

✪ **Boundaries and Expectations**—Young people need the positive influence of peers and adults who encourage them to be and do their best. Youth also need clear rules about appropriate behavior and consistent, reasonable consequences for breaking those rules.

☯ **Constructive Use of Time**—Young people need opportunities—outside of school—to learn and develop new skills and interests and to spend enjoyable time interacting with other youth and adults.

The next four categories reflect internal values, skills, and beliefs that young people also need to develop to fully engage with and function in the world around them:

💡 **Commitment to Learning**—Young people need a variety of learning experiences, including the desire for academic success, a sense of the lasting importance of learning, and a belief in their own abilities.

😊 **Positive Values**—Young people need to develop strong guiding values or principles, including caring about others, having high standards for personal character, and believing in protecting their own well-being.

☺ **Social Competencies**—Young people need to develop the skills to interact effectively with others, to make difficult decisions and choices, and to cope with new situations.

👍 **Positive Identity**—Young people need to believe in their own self-worth, to feel that they have control over the things that happen to them, and to have a sense of purpose in life as well as a positive view of the future.

For a list of all 40 of the Developmental Assets, visit www.search-institute.org.